C Programming for the Absolute Beginner,

Second Edition

Michael Vine

COURSE TECHNOLOGY
CENGAGE Learning™

Australia • Brazil • Japan • Korea • Mexico • Singapore • Spain • United Kingdom • United States

COURSE TECHNOLOGY
CENGAGE Learning™

Publisher and General Manager, Course Technology PTR: Stacy L. Hiquet

Associate Director of Marketing: Sarah O'Donnell

Manager of Editorial Services: Heather Talbot

Marketing Manager: Mark Hughes

Acquisitions Editor: Mitzi Koontz

Project Editor: Jenny Davidson

Technical Reviewer: Greg Perry

PTR Editorial Services Coordinator: Erin Johnson

Copy Editor: Heather Urschel

Interior Layout Tech: Value-Chain

Cover Designer: Mike Tanamachi

Indexer: Kevin Broccoli

Proofreader: Sandi Wilson

For product information and technology assistance, contact us at **Cengage Learning Customer & Sales Support, 1-800-354-9706**

For permission to use material from this text or product, submit all requests online at **cengage.com/permissions** Further permissions questions can be emailed to **permissionrequest@cengage.com**

All other trademarks are the property of their respective owners.

Library of Congress Control Number: 2007935959

ISBN-10: 1-59863-480-1
ISBN-13: 978-1-59863-480-8

Course Technology
25 Thomson Place
Boston, MA 02210
USA

Cengage Learning is a leading provider of customized learning solutions with office locations around the globe, including Singapore, the United Kingdom, Australia, Mexico, Brazil, and Japan. Locate your local office at: **international.cengage.com/region**

Cengage Learning products are represented in Canada by Nelson Education, Ltd.

For your lifelong learning solutions, visit **courseptr.com**

Visit our corporate website at **cengage.com**

Printed in the United States of America
6 7 8 9 10 16 15 14 13 12

To my son, Spencer—Go Bruins!

ACKNOWLEDGMENTS

Writing a book is not easy, especially a technical programming book. It takes many great, patient, and talented people to write, edit, design, market, finance, and produce a book. Without the assistance of Mitzi Koontz, Jenny Davidson, and Heather Urschel, it would be impossible for me to share with you my knowledge of programming in such a professional and fun manner. I would also like to give special thanks to our technical editor, Greg Perry, who is a true C expert. For two editions now, Greg has kept me honest and accurate in the complicated and often misunderstood world of C programming. Thanks, Greg!

ABOUT THE AUTHOR

Michael Vine has taught computer programming, web design, and database classes at Indiana University/Purdue University in Indianapolis, IN, and at MTI College of Business and Technology in Sacramento, CA. Michael has over 13 years' experience in the information technology profession. He currently works full-time in a *Fortune* 100 company as an IT Project Manager overseeing the development of enterprise data warehouses.

TABLE OF CONTENTS

Chapter 3 CONDITIONS... 49

INTRODUCTION

C is a powerful procedural-based programming language developed in 1972 by Dennis Ritchie within the halls of Bell Telephone Laboratories. The C programming language was originally developed for use with the UNIX platform and has since spread to many other systems and applications. C has influenced a number of other programming languages, including C++ and Java.

Beginning programmers, especially those enrolled in computer science and engineering majors, need to build a solid foundation of operating systems, hardware, and application development concepts. Numerous learning institutions accomplish this by teaching their students how to program in C so that they may progress to advanced concepts and other languages built upon C.

Many students of C will rightly admit that it's not an easy language to learn, but fortunately Course Technology PTR's *Absolute Beginner* series' professional insight, clear explanations, examples, and pictures, make learning C easy and fun. Each chapter contains programming challenges, a chapter review, and a complete program that uses chapter-based concepts to construct an easily built application.

To work through this book in its entirety, you should have access to a computer with a C compiler such as gcc and at least one text editor like the ones found on UNIX (e.g., vi, vim, Pico, nano, or Emacs) or Microsoft Windows (e.g., Notepad).

What You'll Find in This Book

To learn how to program a computer, you must acquire a progression of skills. If you have never programmed at all, you will probably find it easiest to go through the chapters in order. Programming is not a skill you can learn by reading. You have to write programs to learn. This book has been designed to make the process reasonably painless and hopefully fun.

Each chapter begins with a brief introduction to chapter-based concepts. Once inside the chapter, you'll look at a series of programming concepts and small programs that illustrate each of the major points of the chapter. Finally, you'll put these concepts together to build a complete program at the end of the chapter. All of the programs are short enough that you can type them in yourself (which is a great way to look closely at code), but they are also available via the publisher's website (www.courseptr.com/downloads). Located at the end of every chapter is a summary that outlines key concepts learned. Use the summaries to refresh your memory on important concepts. In addition to summaries, each chapter contains programming challenges that will help you learn and cement chapter-based concepts.

Throughout the book, I'll throw in a few other tidbits, notably the following:

 These are good ideas that experienced programmers like to pass on.

 These are areas where it's easy to make a mistake.

SIDEBAR

As you examine concepts in this book, I'll show you how the concepts are used beyond beginning programming or in the real world.

WHO THIS BOOK IS FOR

This book was designed with the absolute beginner in mind. This book is not for experienced C programmers wanting to learn object-oriented programming (OOP) with C++ or advanced C data structures, such as linked lists.

This book is for you if:

- You're a college or high school student studying beginning programming with C.
- You're an experienced programmer in other high-level languages, such as Visual Basic, VBA, HTML, or JavaScript, and you are looking to add C to your repertoire.
- You're a programming hobbyist/enthusiast looking to learn C on your own.
- You're interested in learning C++, C#, or Java and you were told to learn C first.
- You've always wanted to learn how to program and have chosen C as your first language.

If you fall into any of the preceding categories, I'm sure you will enjoy this book's non-intimidating approach to programming in C. Specifically, I will teach you the basics of C programming using non-graphical text editors and the ANSI C compiler gcc. You will learn fundamental programming concepts such as variables, conditions, loops, arrays, structures, and file I/O that can be useful in learning any programming language. Of course, you will also learn some C-specific topics such as pointers and dynamic memory allocation, which make the C language unique and oh so powerful.

GETTING STARTED WITH C PROGRAMMING

Welcome to *C Programming for the Absolute Beginner, Second Edition*! Whether you're a computer technology student, self-taught programmer, or seasoned software engineer, you should consider C an essential building block to your programming foundation. After learning C you will have a broader understanding of operating system concepts, memory management, and other high-level programming languages.

Throughout this book I will guide you through a series of examples designed to teach you the basics of C programming. I assume you have no prior experience with C programming or beginning computer science concepts. There are no prerequisites for this book (including advanced math concepts), although I will assume you already have a basic understanding of at least one Microsoft or UNIX-based operating system and text editor.

If you already have some prior programming experience with other languages, such as Java, Visual Basic, PowerBuilder, or COBOL, you will still benefit from this book. I hope after reading *C Programming for the Absolute Beginner, Second Edition* you will continue to find this text a useful C programming reference.

I will cover the following topics in this chapter:

- Installing and configuring the Cygwin environment
- `main()` function
- Keywords
- Comments
- Program statements
- Directives
- gcc compiler
- How to debug C programs

INSTALLING AND CONFIGURING THE CYGWIN ENVIRONMENT

The minimum requirements for learning how to program in C are access to a computer, a text editor, C libraries, and a C compiler. Throughout this book I will use a simple text editor to write C programs. Unlike many high-level programming languages (think Visual Basic or C#), the C language doesn't require a high-end graphical user interface, which in my opinion gets in the way of beginners who want to learn programming. For example, the beginning programmer is so busy messing with a graphical user interface's command buttons and tool-boxes that the concept of a variable or loop becomes secondary, whereas those concepts should be the PRIMARY concern for the beginning programmer.

There are a number of free C compilers and text editors that you can use and, of course, there are many more that cost money. If you already have access to these tools, you can skip this installation section. But if not, my friends at Cygwin have cleverly developed a simple, yet robust Linux-like environment for Win-tel (Microsoft Windows–Intel) platforms that includes many free software packages, such as a C compiler called gcc, text editors, and other common utilities. You can download Cygwin's free software components from their website at http://www.Cygwin.com.

The Cygwin setup process is very easy, but if you have questions or issues you can visit the online user guide via http://cygwin.com/cygwin-ug-net/cygwin-ug-net.html. Once installed, you will have access to many UNIX-based utilities that can be accessed via a UNIX shell or the Windows command prompt.

A minimum of 400MB of free hard drive space is required for installation (more or less depending on the components selected). To install Cygwin and its associated components, download the setup file from the aforementioned website or run the setup file directly from Cygwin's website (http://www.cygwin.com/setup.exe). Follow the setup screens until you get to the Cygwin Setup – Select Packages window, from which you can select the components you want to install. As of this writing, the default components selected plus the "gcc-core: C Compiler" installation component will be enough to follow this book in its entirety. Note that the gcc-core: C Compiler component is not selected by default. To select this component, click the plus sign (+) next to the Devel category and scroll down until you find the gcc-core: C Compiler component. Click the word "skip" to select the component for installation.

> If you want to select a component not already selected by default, click the word "skip" in the Select Packages installation window to select a Cygwin component to install.

After successfully installing the Cygwin environment, you will have access to a simulated UNIX operating system through a UNIX shell. To start the UNIX shell, simply find the Cygwin shortcut located on the desktop or through the program group found in the Start menu.

After starting the program, the Cygwin UNIX shell should resemble Figure 1.1

FIGURE 1.1

Launching the Cygwin UNIX shell.

Note the syntax used for the UNIX command prompt in Figure 1.1—yours will differ slightly.

```
Administrator@MVINE ~
$
```

The first line shows that you are logged into the UNIX shell as Administrator (default login name) at your computer (MVINE is the name of my PC). The next line starts with a dollar sign ($). This is the UNIX command prompt from where you will execute UNIX commands.

Depending on your specific installation (Cygwin version) and configuration (components selected) of Cygwin, you may need to have Cygwin's bin directory, referenced next, added to your system's PATH environment variable.

```
c:\cygwin\bin
```

The PATH environment variable is used by Cygwin to find executable files to run. If you are using a Microsoft-based operating system, you can edit the PATH variable in a couple of ways. One trick is to launch a Microsoft-based command shell (DOS window) by typing the keyword cmd from the Run dialog box accessed via the Start menu. From the c:\ prompt (in the command shell), type:

```
PATH %PATH%;c:\cygwin\bin
```

This command appends c:\cygwin\bin to the end of the current PATH variable without overwriting it. To verify the command was successful, simply type the keyword PATH from the same Microsoft-based command shell window. Note that a semicolon separates each distinct directory structure in the PATH's value. If necessary, consult your system's documentation for more information on environment variables and specifically updating the PATH system variable.

main() FUNCTION

In this section, I'll start with the beginning of every C program, the main() function. Let's first, however, talk philosophically about what a function is. From a programming perspective, *functions* allow you to group a logical series of activities, or *program statements*, under one name. For example, suppose I want to create a function called bakeCake. My algorithm for baking a cake might look like this:

> Mix wet ingredients in mixing bowl
> Combine dry ingredients
> Spoon batter into greased baking pan
> Bake cake at 350 degrees for 30 minutes

Anyone reading my code will see my function called bakeCake and know right away that I'm trying to bake cakes.

Functions are typically not static, meaning they are living and breathing entities, again philosophically, that take in and pass back information. Thus, my bakeCake function would take in a list of ingredients to bake (called *parameters*) and return back a finished cake (called a *value*).

ALGORITHMS

An *algorithm* is a finite step-by-step process for solving a problem. It can be as simple as a recipe to bake a cake, or as complicated as the process to implement an autopilot system for a 747 jumbo jet.

Algorithms generally start off with a problem statement. It is this problem statement that programmers use to formulate the process for solving the problem. Keep in mind that the process of building algorithms and algorithm analysis occurs before any program code has been written.

The main() function is like any other programming function in that it groups like activities and can take in parameters (information) and pass back values (again, information). What makes the main() function unique from other functions, however, is that the values it returns are returned to the operating system. Other functions that you will use and create in this book return values back to the calling C statement inside the main() function.

In this book, I will use main() functions that are void of parameters (functions that do not take parameters) and do not return values.

```
main()
{

}
```

As the preceding example shows, the main() function begins with the keyword main and is followed by two empty parentheses (). The parentheses are used to encompass parameters to be passed to the main() function.

 C is a case-sensitive programming language. For example, the function names main(), Main(), and MAIN() are not the same. It takes extra computing resources to NOT be case-sensitive as input devices such as keyboards distinguish between cases.

Following the parentheses are two braces. The first brace denotes the beginning of a logical programming block and the last brace denotes the end of a logical programming block. Each function implementation requires that you use a beginning brace, {, and a closing brace, }.

The following program code demonstrates a complete, simple C program. From this code, you will learn how single program statements come together to form a complete C program.

```
/* C Programming for the Absolute Beginner */

//by Michael Vine

#include <stdio.h>

main()
{
    printf("\nC you later\n");
}
```

When the preceding program is compiled and run, it outputs the text "C you later" to the computer screen, as shown in Figure 1.2.

FIGURE 1.2

C program with standard output.

Review the sample program code in Figure 1.3; you can see the many components that comprise a small C program.

FIGURE 1.3

Building blocks of a simple C program.

The remainder of this chapter will cover these components and how each is used to build a simple C program.

COMMENTS

Comments are an integral part of program code in any programming language. Comments help to identify program purpose and explain complex routines. They can be valuable to you as the programmer and to other programmers looking at your code.

In the following line of code, the text `C Programming for the Absolute Beginner` is ignored by the compiler because it is surrounded with the character sets /* and */.

```
/* C Programming for the Absolute Beginner */
```

The character set /* signifies the beginning of a comment block; the character set */ identifies the end of a comment block. These character sets are not required to be on the same line and can be used to create both single-line and multi-line comments. To demonstrate, the following block of code shows the usefulness of multi-line commenting.

```
/*      C Programming for the Absolute Beginner
        Chapter 1 - Getting Started with C Programming
        By Michael Vine
*/
```

Your C program may not compile correctly if you leave one of the comment character sets out or if you reverse the characters. For example, the following code segment leaves out a comment character set and will not compile.

```
/* C Programming for the Absolute Beginner
```

The next line of code also will not compile because comment character sets have been incorrectly ordered.

```
*/ C Programming for the Absolute Beginner */
```

You can also create quick one-line comments with the character set //. The next line of code demonstrates this.

```
//by Michael Vine
```

 If your C compiler supports C++, which gcc does, you can use the single line // character set for one-line commenting. Though unlikely, be aware that not all C compilers support the single line character set.

Any characters read after the character set // are ignored by the compiler for that line only. To create a multi-line comment block with character set //, you will need the comment characters in front of each line. For example, the following code creates a multi-line comment block.

```
//C Programming for the Absolute Beginner
//Chapter 1 - Getting Started with C Programming
//By Michael Vine
```

KEYWORDS

There are 32 words defined as keywords in the standard ANSI C programming language. These keywords have predefined uses and cannot be used for any other purpose in a C program. These keywords are used by the compiler, in this case gcc, as an aid to building the program. Note that these keywords must always be written in lowercase (see Table 1.1).

TABLE 1.1 C LANGUAGE KEYWORDS	
Keyword	**Description**
auto	Defines a local variable as having a local lifetime
break	Passes control out of the programming construct
case	Branch control
char	Basic data type
const	Unmodifiable value
continue	Passes control to loop's beginning
default	Branch control
do	Do While loop
double	Floating-point data type
else	Conditional statement
enum	Defines a group of constants of type int
extern	Indicates an identifier as defined elsewhere
float	Floating-point data type
for	For loop
goto	Transfers program control unconditionally
if	Conditional statement
int	Basic data type
long	Type modifier
register	Stores the declared variable in a CPU register

```
return          Exits the function
short           Type modifier
signed          Type modifier
sizeof          Returns expression or type size
static          Preserves variable value after its scope ends
struct          Groups variables into a single record
switch          Branch control
typedef         Creates a new type
union           Groups variables that occupy the same storage space
unsigned        Type modifier
void            Empty data type
volatile        Allows a variable to be changed by a background routine
while           Repeats program execution while the condition is true
```

Be aware that in addition to the list of keywords above, your C language compiler may define a few more. If it does, they will be listed in the documentation that came with your compiler.

As you progress through this book, I will show you how to use many of the aforementioned C language keywords.

PROGRAM STATEMENTS

Many lines in C programs are considered *program statements*, which serve to control program execution and functionality. Many of these program statements must end with a statement terminator. Statement terminators are simply semicolons (;). The next line of code, which includes the printf() function, demonstrates a program statement with a statement terminator.

```
printf("\nC you later\n");
```

Some common program statements that do not require the use of statement terminators are the following:

- Comments
- Preprocessor directives (for example, #include or #define)
- Begin and end program block identifiers
- Function definition beginnings (for example, main())

The preceding program statements don't require the semicolon (;) terminator because they are not executable C statements or function calls. Only C statements that perform work during program execution require the semicolons.

A function commonly used for displaying output to the computer screen is the `printf()` function. As shown next, the `printf()` function is used to write the text "C you later" to the standard output (demonstrated in Figure 1.2).

```
printf("\nC you later\n");
```

Like most functions, the `printf()` function takes a value as a parameter. (I'll talk more about functions in Chapter 5, "Structured Programming.") Any text you want to display in the standard output must be enclosed by quotation marks.

For the most part, characters or text that you want to appear on-screen are put inside quotation marks, with the exception of escape characters or escape sequences. The backslash character (\) is the *escape character*. When the `printf()` statement shown above is executed, the program looks forward to the next character that follows the backslash. In this case, the next character is the character n. Together, the backslash (\) and n characters make up an *escape sequence*.

ESCAPE SEQUENCES

Escape sequences are specially sequenced characters used to format output.

This particular escape sequence (\n) tells the program to add a new line. Take a look at the following program statement. How many new lines are added to standard output with this one `printf()` function?

```
printf("\nC you later\n");
```

This `printf()` function adds two new lines for formatting purposes. Before any text is shown, the program outputs a new line. After the text is written to standard output, in this case the computer screen, another new line is written.

Table 1.2 describes some common escape sequences.

TABLE 1.2   COMMON ESCAPE SEQUENCES

Escape Sequence	Purpose
\n	Creates a new line
\t	Moves the cursor to the next tab
\r	Moves the cursor to the beginning of the current line
\\	Inserts a backslash
\"	Inserts a double quote
\'	Inserts a single quote

Escape Sequence \n

As depicted in Figures 1.4 and 1.5, escape sequence \n can be used in a multitude of ways to format output.

FIGURE 1.4

Using escape sequence \n with one printf() function to generate multiple lines.

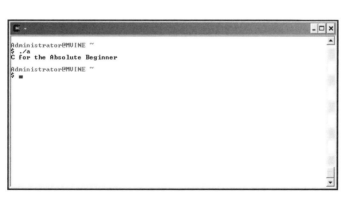

FIGURE 1.5

Using escape sequence \n with multiple printf() functions to generate a single line.

The following code segment generates three separate lines with only one `printf()` function.

```
printf("line 1\nline2\nline3\n");
```

The next code segment demonstrates how escape sequence \n can be used with multiple `printf()` statements to create a single line of output.

```
printf("C ");
printf("for the ");
printf("Absolute Beginner\n");
```

Escape Sequence \t

Escape sequence \t moves the cursor to the next tab space. This escape sequence is useful for formatting output in many ways. For example, a common formatting desire is to create columns in your output, as the following program statements demonstrate.

```
printf("\nSun\tMon\tTue\tWed\tThu\tFri\tSat\n");
printf("\t\t\t\t1\t2\t3\n");
printf("4\t5\t6\t7\t8\t9\t10\n");
printf("11\t12\t13\t14\t15\t16\t17\n");
printf("18\t19\t20\t21\t22\t23\t24\n");
printf("25\t26\t27\t28\t29\t30\t31\n");
```

As shown in Figure 1.6, the preceding program statements create formatted columns that display a sample calendar month.

FIGURE 1.6

Demonstrating the use of tab spaces and columns with escape sequence \t.

Escape Sequence \r

You may find the escape sequence \r useful for some formatting tasks when the cursor's position is of importance, especially with printed output because a printer can overwrite text already printing. The following program code demonstrates how it works; the output is shown in Figure 1.7.

```
printf("This escape sequence moves the cursor ");
printf("to the beginning of this line\r");
```

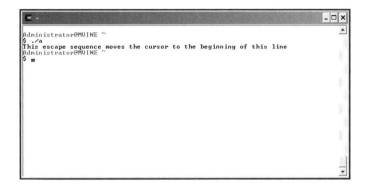

FIGURE 1.7

Demonstrating escape sequence \r.

Escape Sequence \\

Escape sequence \\ inserts a backslash into your text. This may seem unnecessary at first, but remember that whenever the program reads a backslash in a printf() function, it expects to see a valid escape character right after it. In other words, the backslash character (\) is a special character in the printf() function; if you need to display a backslash in your text, you must use this escape sequence.

The following program statement demonstrates escape sequence \\. The output is shown in Figure 1.8.

```
printf("c:\\cygwin\\bin must be in your system path");
```

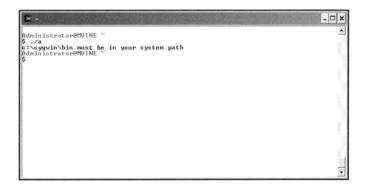

FIGURE 1.8

Demonstrating escape sequence \\.

Escape Sequence \"

Another reserved character in the printf() function is the double quote (") character. To insert a quote into your outputted text, use the escape sequence \" as demonstrated in the following program statement. The output is shown in Figure 1.9.

```
printf("\"This is quoted text\"");
```

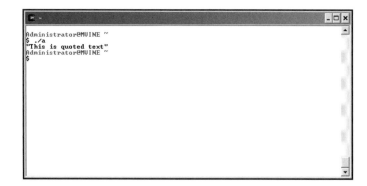

FIGURE 1.9

Creating quotes
with escape
sequence \".

Escape Sequence \'

Similar to the double quote escape sequence (\") is the single quote (also called an apostrophe) escape sequence (\'). To insert a single quote into your outputted text, use the escape sequence \' as demonstrated in the following program statement and in Figure 1.10.

```
printf("\nA single quote looks like \'\n");
```

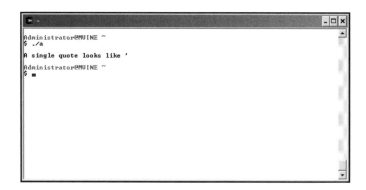

FIGURE 1.10

Inserting single
quotes
with escape
sequence \'.

DIRECTIVES

Here's another look at the sample program shown earlier in the chapter.

```
/* C Programming for the Absolute Beginner */

//by Michael Vine

#include <stdio.h>

main()
{

   printf("\nC you later\n");

}
```

Notice the program statement that begins with the pound sign (#):

```
#include <stdio.h>
```

When the C preprocessor encounters the pound sign, it performs certain actions depending on the *directive* that occurs prior to compiling. In the preceding example, I told the preprocessor to include the `stdio.h` library with my program.

The name `stdio.h` is short for *standard input output header file*. It contains links to various standard C library functions, such as `printf()`. Excluding this preprocessor directive will not have an adverse affect when compiling or running your program. However, including the header file allows the compiler to better help you determine error locations. You should always add a directive to include any library header files that you use in your C programs.

In the chapters to come, you will learn other common library functions, how to use other preprocessor directives such as macros, and how to build your own library files.

GCC COMPILER

The gcc compiler is an ANSI standard C compiler. A C program goes through a lot of steps prior to becoming a running or executing program. The gcc compiler performs a number of tasks for you. Most notable are the following:

- Preprocesses the program code and looks for various directives.
- Generates error codes and messages, if applicable.

- Compiles program code into an object code and stores it temporarily on disk.
- Links any necessary library to the object code and creates an executable file and stores it on disk.

ANSI

ANSI is an abbreviation for the *American National Standard for Information Systems*. ANSI's common goal is to provide computing standards for people who use information systems.

Use the .c extension when creating and saving C programs. This extension is the standard naming convention for programs created in C. To create a new C program, invoke a text editor such as nano or VIM as shown next.

```
nano hello.c
vim hello.c
```

 nano is another common UNIX-based text editor that comes with the Cygwin software package. From an end-user perspective, it is much more intuitive and easier to use than VIM, but it does not have the amount of functionality as VIM. Though not selected in a default installation of Cygwin, nano and other text editors can be selected during installation via the Select Packages window.

Both of the preceding command statements open a text editor and create a new file called hello.c.

Once you've created a C program using an editor, such as nano or VIM, you are ready to compile your program using gcc.

From the Cygwin UNIX shell, type the following:

```
gcc hello.c
```

If your program compiles successfully, gcc will create a new executable file called a.exe.

 If you are unsuccessful in running your compiled program, verify that the %drive %:\cygwin\bin (where %drive% is the drive letter of where Cygwin is installed) directory structure has been added to your system path variable.

a.exe is the default name for all C programs compiled with this version of gcc. If you're programming under a different version of gcc on a UNIX operating system, the file name may be a.out.

Every time you compile a C program with gcc, it overwrites the previous data contained in the a.exe file. You can correct this by supplying gcc with an option to specify a unique name for your executable file. The syntax for specifying a unique executable name is as follows.

```
gcc programName -o executableName
```

The `programName` keyword is the name of your C program, the `-o` (letter o) option tells gcc that you will specify a unique compile name, and the `executableName` keyword is the desired output name. Here's another example that uses actual file names.

```
gcc hello.c -o hello.exe
```

You can find a wealth of information on the gcc program by accessing gcc's man pages (the online manual pages for UNIX commands) from the UNIX prompt as shown here.

```
man gcc
```

To execute your program from the Cygwin UNIX prompt, type in the following:

```
./hello
```

Unlike Windows, the UNIX shell does not by default look in the current directory when trying to execute a program. By preceding the name of your compiled program with the `./` character sequence, you're telling the UNIX shell to look for the compiled C program, in this case `hello`, in the current directory.

If you're using a Microsoft Windows system, you can also execute your program from a Microsoft-based command shell often referred to as a DOS prompt (provided you're in the working directory) by simply typing in the name of the program.

Note that in both cases it is not necessary to follow the compiled program name with the file extension `.exe`.

How to Debug C Programs

If your program compiles, exits, or executes abnormally, there is almost certainly an error (a *bug*) in your program. A fair amount of your programming time will be spent finding and removing these bugs. This section provides some tips to help you get started. Remember, though, that debugging is as much art as it is computer science and, of course, the more you practice programming the easier debugging will become!

Often a program will compile and execute just fine, but with results you did not expect. For example, the following program and its output shown in Figure 1.11 compiles and executes without error, but the output is unreadable, or in other words, not what I expected.

```c
#include <stdio.h>

main()
{
    printf("Chapter 1 - Getting Started with C Programming");
    printf("This is an example of a format bug.");
    printf("The format issue can be corrected by using");
    printf(" the \n and \\ escape sequences");

}
```

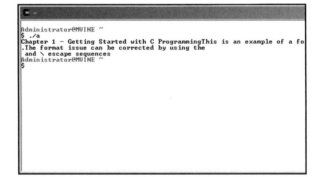

FIGURE 1.11

A sample format bug.

Can you see where the format issue or issues are? What's missing and where should the correction or corrections be placed? The next block of code and its output in Figure 1.12 corrects the format issues with appropriately placed escape sequences.

```c
#include <stdio.h>

main()
{
    printf("Chapter 1 - Getting Started with C Programming\n");
     printf("This is an example of a format bug.\n");
     printf("The format issue can be corrected by using");
     printf(" the \\n and \\\\ escape sequences");

}
```

FIGURE 1.12

Correcting format
bugs with
appropriately
placed \n and \\
escape sequences.

Format issues are common in beginning programming and are typically quickly resolved by practicing the printf() function and the various escape sequences.

Another common bug type is a logic error, including a loop that doesn't exit when expected, an incorrect mathematical equation, or perhaps a flawed test for equality (condition). The first step in debugging a logic error is to find the first line where the program bug exists. One way of doing this is through print statements, using the printf() function, scattered through your code. For example, you might do something like this in your source code:

```
anyFunction(int x, int y)
{
    printf("Entering anyFunction()\n"); fflush(stdout);
    ---- lots of your code here ------
    printf("Exiting anyFunction()\n");  fflush(stdout);
}
```

The fflush() function ensures that the print statement is sent to your screen immediately, and you should use it if you're using printf()'s for debugging purposes. The stdout parameter passed to the fflush() function is the standard output, generally the computer screen.

After you have narrowed down the line or function where your logic error occurs, the next step is to find out the value of your variables at that time. You can also use the printf() function to print variable values, which will aid you greatly in determining the source of abnormal program behavior. Displaying variable values using the printf() function will be discussed in Chapter 2 in detail.

Remember, after you fix any bug, you must recompile your program, run it, and debug it again if necessary.

Beginning programmers will, more often than not, encounter compile errors rather than logic errors, which are generally the result of syntax issues such as missing identifiers and terminators or invalid directives, escape sequences, and comment blocks.

Debugging compile errors can be a daunting task, especially when you see 50 or more errors on the computer screen. One important thing to remember is that a single error at the top of your program can cause cascading errors during compile time. So it goes without saying that the best place to start debugging compile errors is with the first error on the list! In the next few sections, you'll explore some of the more common compile errors beginning C Programmers experience.

Common Error #1: Missing Program Block Identifiers

If you forget to insert a beginning or a corresponding ending program block identifier ({ or }), you will see error messages similar to those in Figure 1.13. In the example below, I have intentionally neglected to use the beginning program block identifier ({) after the main() function name.

```
#include <stdio.h>


main()


  printf("Welcome to C Programming\n");


}
```

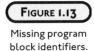

Missing program
block identifiers.

Yikes! Figure 1.13 shows lot of errors for simply forgetting to use the beginning program block identifier ({). When debugging compile errors, remember to simply start with the first error, shown next, which tells me that I have an error right before the printf() function. You will find that after solving the first error, many of the remaining errors no longer exist.

```
hello.c:8: error: parse error before "printf"
```

Another clue that will help you is to look at the line number of the program statement referenced in the compile error. In this case it's line number eight, hello.c:8:, which is the line number of the printf() function in question. It's important to recognize that the issue is *not* with the print statement, but as the compile error suggests, an issue exists before it.

Common Error #2: Missing Statement Terminators

Figure 1.13 depicts a common error message generated by a few common scenarios. This type of parse error can be generated for a couple of reasons. In addition to missing program block identifiers, parse errors can occur because of missing statement terminators (semicolons).

Figure 1.14 depicts a bug in the following program. Can you see where the bug exists?

```c
#include <stdio.h>

main()
{
  printf("Welcome to C Programming\n")
}
```

FIGURE 1.14

Program statements with missing terminators.

Parse errors occur because the C compiler is unable to determine the end of a program statement such as print statement. In the example shown in Figure 1.14, the C compiler (gcc) tells us that on line 10 a parse error exists before the closing brace.

Common Error #3: Invalid Preprocessor Directives

If you type an invalid preprocessor directive, such as misspelling a library name, you will receive an error message similar to Figure 1.15.

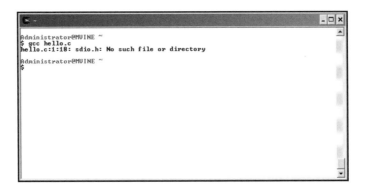

FIGURE 1.15

Misspelling library names.

The following program block with a misspelled library name in the preprocessor directive caused the error generated in Figure 1.15. Can you see the error?

```
#include <sdio.h>

main()

{
  printf("Welcome to C Programming\n");
}
```

This error was caused because the library file sdio.h does not exist. The library name for standard input output should be spelled stdio.h.

Common Error #4: Invalid Escape Sequences

When using escape sequences it is common to use invalid characters or invalid character sequences. For example, Figure 1.16 depicts an error generated by an invalid escape sequence.

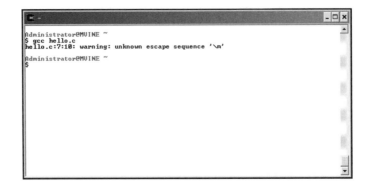

FIGURE 1.16

Invalid escape sequences.

As shown in Figure 1.16, the gcc compiler is more specific about this error. Specifically, it notes that the error is on line 7 and that it is an unknown escape sequence.

Can you identify the invalid escape sequence in the following program?

```
#include <stdio.h>

main()

{
  printf("Welcome to C Programming\m");
}
```

Replacing the invalid escape sequence \m with a valid sequence such as \n will correct the problem.

Common Error #5: Invalid Comment Blocks

As mentioned earlier in the comment section of this chapter, invalid comment blocks can generate compile errors, as shown in Figure 1.17.

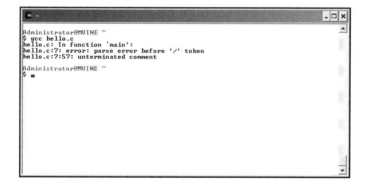

FIGURE 1.17

Errors generated by invalid comment blocks.

```
#include <stdio.h>

main()

{
  */ This demonstrates a common error with comment blocks /*
  printf("Welcome to C Programming\n");
}
```

A simple correction to the comment block, shown next, will solve the issue and allow the program to compile successfully.

```
/* This corrects the previous comment block error */
```

SUMMARY

- Functions allow you to group a logical series of activities, or program statements, under one name.
- Functions can take in and pass back information.
- An algorithm is a finite step-by-step process for solving a problem.
- Each function implementation requires that you use a beginning brace ({) and a closing brace (}).
- Comments help to identify program purpose and explain complex routines.
- The character set /* signifies the beginning of a comment block and the character set */ identifies the end of a comment block.
- There are 32 words defined as keywords in the standard ANSI C programming language; these keywords have predefined uses and cannot be used for any other purpose in a C program.
- Most program statements control program execution and functionality and may require a program statement terminator (;).
- Program statements that do not require a terminator include preprocessor directives, comment blocks, and function headers.
- The printf() function is used to display output to the computer screen.
- When combined with the backslash (\), special characters such as n make up an escape sequence.
- The library name stdio.h is short for standard input output and contains links to various standard C library functions, such as printf().
- C compilers such as gcc preprocess program code, generate error codes and messages if applicable, compile program code into object code, and link any necessary libraries.
- Compile errors are generally the result of syntax issues, including missing identifiers and terminators, or invalid directives, escape sequences, and comment blocks.
- A single error at the top of your program can cause cascading errors during compile time.
- The best place to start debugging compile errors is with the first error.

CHALLENGES

1. Study the VIM Quick Guide as described in Appendix B.
2. Study the nano Quick Guide as described in Appendix C.
3. Create a program that prints your name.
4. Create a program that uses escape sequence \" to print your favorite quote.
5. Create a program that uses escape sequence \\ to print the following directory structure: `c:\cygwin\home\administrator`.
6. Write a program that prints a diamond as demonstrated next.

```
        *
     *     *
   *           *
 *               *
   *           *
     *     *
        *
```

7. Create a calendar program using the current month (similar to the one shown in Figure 1.6).

PRIMARY DATA TYPES

This chapter investigates essential computer memory concepts, as well as how to get information from users and store it as data using C language data types. In addition to beginning data types, you will also learn how to display variable contents using the `printf()` function and to manipulate data stored in variables using basic arithmetic. Specifically, this chapter covers the following topics:

- Memory concepts
- Data types
- Initializing variables and the assignment operator
- Printing variable contents
- Constants
- Programming conventions and styles
- `scanf()`
- Arithmetic in C
- Operator precedence

MEMORY CONCEPTS

A computer's memory is somewhat like a human's, in that a computer has both short-term and long-term memory. A computer's long-term memory is called *nonvolatile* memory and is generally associated with mass storage devices, such as hard drives, large disk arrays, optical storage (CD/DVD), and of course portable storage devices such as USB flash or key drives. In Chapters 10 and 11, you will learn how to use nonvolatile memory for storing data.

This chapter concentrates on a computer's short-term, or *volatile,* memory. Volatile memory loses its data when power is removed from the computer. It's commonly referred to as RAM (random access memory).

RAM is comprised of fixed-size cells with each cell number referenced through an address. Programmers commonly reference memory cells through the use of variables. There are many types of variables, depending on the programming language, but all variables share similar characteristics, as described in Table 2.1.

TABLE 2.1 COMMON VARIABLE CHARACTERISTICS	
Variable Attribute	**Description**
Name	The name of the variable used to reference data in program code
Type	The data type of the variable (number, character, and so on)
Value	The data value assigned to the memory location
Address	The address assigned to a variable, which points to a memory cell location

Using the attributes defined in Table 2.1, Figure 2.1 depicts the graphical relationship for some common data types. Note that the letters and numbers in the "Memory Address" column in Figure 2.1, such as FFF4, represent memory locations in the hexadecimal numbering system. The hexadecimal numbering system is sometimes used in advanced C programming to reference concise memory addresses, such as during system-level programming.

Variable Name	Value	Type	Memory Address
Operand1	29	integer	FFF4
Result	756.21	float	FHH6
Initial	M	character	FHF2

FIGURE 2.1

Depicting common variable attributes and sample values.

DATA TYPES

You will discover many data types in your programming career, such as numbers, dates, strings, Boolean, arrays, objects, and data structures. Although this book covers some of the aforementioned data types in later chapters, this chapter will concentrate on the following primary data types:

- Integers
- Floating-point numbers
- Characters

Integers

Integers are whole numbers that represent positive and negative numbers, such as −3, −2, −1, 0, 1, 2, and 3, but not decimal or fractional numbers.

Integer data types hold a maximum of four bytes of information and are declared with the int (short for integer) keyword, as shown in the following line of code.

```
int x;
```

In C, you can declare more than one variable on the same line using a single int declaration statement with each variable name separated by commas, as demonstrated next.

```
int x, y, z;
```

The preceding variable declaration declares three integer variables named x, y, and z. Remember from Chapter 1 that executable program statements such as a print statement or in this case a variable declaration require a statement terminator (;).

Floating-Point Numbers

Floating-point numbers are all numbers, including signed and unsigned decimal and fractional numbers. Signed numbers include positive and negative numbers whereas unsigned numbers can only include positive values. Examples of floating-point numbers are shown in the following list.

- 09.4543
- 3428.27
- 112.34329
- -342.66
- -55433.33281

Use the keyword `float` to declare floating-point numbers, as shown next.

```
float operand1;
float operand2;
float result;
```

The preceding code declares three floating-point variable data types called `operand1`, `operand2`, and `result`.

Characters

Character data types are representations of integer values known as *character codes*. For example, the character code 90 represents the letter Z. Note that the letter Z is not the same as the character code 122, which represents the letter z (lowercase letter z).

Characters represent more than just the letters of the alphabet; they also represent numbers 0 through 9, special characters such as the asterisk (*), and keyboard keys such as the Del (delete) key and Esc (escape) key. In all, there are a total of 128 common character codes (0 through 127), which make up the most commonly used characters of a keyboard.

Character codes are most notably organized through the ASCII (American Standard Code for Information Interchange) character set. For a listing of common ASCII character codes, see Appendix D, "Common ASCII Character Codes."

ASCII

ASCII or American Standard Code for Information Interchange is noted for its character set, which uses small integer values to represent character or keyboard values.

In C, character variables are created using the `char` (short for character) keyword as demonstrated next.

```
char firstInitial;
char middleInitial;
char lastInitial;
```

Character data assigned to character variables must be enclosed in single quotes ('), also known as tick marks or apostrophes. As you'll see in the next section, the equal sign (=) is used for assigning data to the character variable.

You cannot assign multiple characters to a single character variable type. When more than one character is needed for storing a single variable, you must use a character array (discussed in Chapter 6, "Arrays") or strings (discussed in Chapter 8, "Strings").

Initializing Variables and the Assignment Operator

When variables are first declared, the program assigns the variable name (address pointer) to an available memory location. It is never safe to assume that the newly assigned variable location is empty. It's possible that the memory location contains previously used data (or garbage). To prevent unwanted data from appearing in your newly created variables, initialize the new variables, as shown below.

```
/* Declare variables */
int x;
char firstInitial;

/* Initialize variables */
x = 0;
firstInitial = '\0';
```

The preceding code declares two variables: one integer and one character data type. After creating the two variables, I initialize them to a particular value. For the integer variable, I assign the value zero (0), and for the character data type, I assign the character set \0, which is known as the NULL character.

Notice that in the character variable data assignment I enclosed the NULL character in single quotes. Single quotes are required when assigning data to the character data type.

The NULL data type is commonly used to initialize memory locations in programming languages, such as C, and relational databases, such as Oracle and SQL Server.

Although NULL data types are a common computer science concept, they can be confusing. Essentially, NULL characters are unknown data types stored in a memory location. However, it is not proper to think of NULL data as empty or void; instead, think of NULL data as simply undefined.

When assigning data to variables such as variable initialization, the equal sign is not used in a comparative sense. In other words, you would not say that x equals 0. Rather, programmers say variable x is taking on the value of 0.

Remember, when assigning data to variables, such as initializing, you refer to the equal sign as an assignment operator, not a comparison operator.

You can also initialize your variables while declaring them, as shown next.

```
int x = 0;
char firstInitial = '\0';
```

The preceding code accomplishes the same tasks in two lines as what the following code accomplishes in four.

```
int x;
char firstInitial;
x = 0;
firstInitial = '\0';
```

PRINTING VARIABLE CONTENTS

To print the contents of variables, use the printf() function with a few new formatting options, as demonstrated in the following code block.

```
#include <stdio.h>

main()

{

    //variable declarations
    int x;
    float y;
    char c;

    //variable initializations
    x = -4443;
    y = 554.21;
    c = 'M';

    //printing variable contents to standard output
    printf("\nThe value of integer variable x is %d", x);
    printf("\nThe value of float variable y is %f", y);
    printf("\nThe value of character variable c is %c\n", c);


}
```

First, I declare three variables (one integer, one float, and one character), and then I initialize each of them. After initializing the variables, I use the printf() function and conversion specifiers (discussed next) to output each variable's contents to the computer screen.

The preceding code is a complete C program that demonstrates many of the topics discussed thus far (its output is shown in Figure 2.2.).

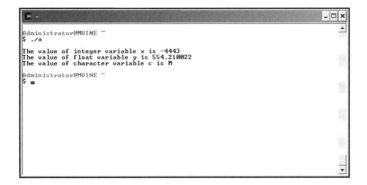

FIGURE 2.2

Printing variable contents.

CONVERSION SPECIFIERS

Because information is stored as unreadable data in the computer's memory, programmers in C must specifically tell input or output functions, such as printf(), how to display the data as information. You can accomplish this seemingly difficult task using character sets known as *conversion specifiers*.

Conversion specifiers are comprised of two characters: The first character is the percent sign (%), and the second is a special character that tells the program how to convert the data. Table 2.2 describes the most common conversion specifiers for the data types discussed in this chapter.

TABLE 2.2 COMMON CONVERSION SPECIFIERS USED WITH PRINTF()	
Conversion Specifier	**Description**
%d	Displays integer value
%f	Displays floating-point numbers
%c	Displays character

Displaying Integer Data Types with printf()

Integer data types can easily be displayed using the %d conversion specifier with a `printf()` statement as shown next.

```
printf("%d", 55);
```

The output of the preceding statement prints the following text:

```
55
```

The %d conversion specifier can also be used to output the contents of a variable declared as integer data type, as demonstrated next.

```
int operand1;
operand1 = 29;
printf("The value of operand1 is %d", operand1);
```

In the preceding statements, I declare a new integer variable called operand1. Next, I assign the number 29 to the newly created variable and display its contents using the `printf()` function with the %d conversion specifier.

Each variable displayed using a `printf()` function must be outside the parentheses and separated with a comma (,).

Displaying Floating-Point Data Types with printf()

To display floating-point numbers, use the %f conversion specifier demonstrated next.

```
printf("%f", 55.55);
```

Here's another example of the %f conversion specifier, which prints the contents of a floating-point variable:

```
float result;
result = 3.123456;
printf("The value of result is %f", result);
```

Although the %f conversion specifier displays floating-point numbers, it may not be enough to display the floating-point number with correct or wanted precision. The following `printf()` function demonstrates the precision problem.

```
printf("%f", 55.55);
```

This `printf()` example outputs a floating-point number with a six-digit precision to the right of the decimal point, as shown next.

```
55.550000
```

To create precision with floating-point numbers, adjust the conversion specifier using numbering schemes between the % sign and the f character conversion specifier.

```
printf("%.1f", 3.123456);
printf("\n%.2f", 3.123456);
printf("\n%.3f", 3.123456);
printf("\n%.4f", 3.123456);
printf("\n%.5f", 3.123456);
printf("\n%.6f", 3.123456);
```

The preceding code block produces the following output:

```
3.1
3.12
3.123
3.1234
3.12345
3.123456
```

Notice that I've included the escape sequence \n in each of the preceding print statements (except the first line of code). Without the new line (\n) escape sequence, each statement's output would generate on the same line, making it difficult to read.

Displaying Character Data Types with printf()

Characters are also easy to display using the %c conversion specifier.

```
printf("%c", 'M');
```

The output of this statement is simply the single letter M. Like the other conversion specifiers, you can output the contents of a character variable data type using the %c conversion specifier and a printf() function as demonstrated next.

```
char firstInitial;
firstInitial = 'S';
printf("The value of firstInitial is %c", firstInitial);
```

You can use multiple conversion specifiers in a single printf() function:

```
char firstInitial, middleInitial, lastInitial;
firstInitial = 'M';
middleInitial = 'A';
lastInitial = 'V';
printf("My Initials are %c.%c.%c.", firstInitial, middleInitial, lastInitial);
```

The output of the preceding program statements is as follows.

```
My Initials are M.A.V.
```

Notice in the statement below that each variable displayed with the `printf()` function is outside the double quotes and separated with a single comma.

```
printf("My Initials are %c.%c.%c.", firstInitial, middleInitial, lastInitial);
```

Text inside of `printf()`'s double quotes is reserved for displayable text, conversion specifiers, and escape sequences.

CONSTANTS

Often referred to as read-only variables, constant data types cannot lose their data values during program execution. They are most commonly used when you need to reuse a common data value without changing it.

Constant data values can be of many data types but must be assigned when the constant is first created, as demonstrated next.

```
const int x = 20;
const float PI = 3.14;
```

Notice that the keyword `const` precedes the data-type name, signaling that this is a read-only variable or constant. You can print the values of constants in the same way that normal variables are printed using conversion specifiers with the `printf()` function as shown in the following program code:

```
#include <stdio.h>

main()

{

    const int x = 20;
    const float PI = 3.14;

    printf("\nConstant values are %d and %.2f\n", x, PI);

}
```

Figure 2.3 demonstrates the output of the preceding code block.

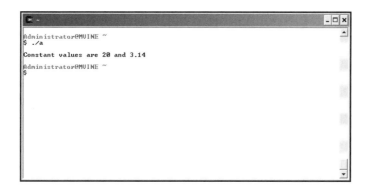

FIGURE 2.3

Printing constant
data-type values.

PROGRAMMING CONVENTIONS AND STYLES

If someone hasn't already mentioned this to you, let me be the first to say that programming
is as much of an art as it is a science! Your programs are a reflection of you and should reveal
a smooth and consistent style that guides the reader's eyes through algorithms and program
flow. Just as a bridge provides function, it can also provide beauty, eye candy for both the
structural engineer as well as the traveler.

You should stick with a style and convention that allow you or someone else to easily read
your code. Once you pick or become comfortable with a programming style, the name of the
game is consistency. In other words, stick with it, don't intermix naming conventions for
variables nor intermingle indenting styles within the same program.

When learning how to program you should specifically consider at least two areas to develop
a consistent programming convention and style.

- White space
- Variable naming conventions

White Space

White space is not often discussed in programming circles as it provides no computing benefits. In fact, the compiler ignores white space, so you're free to treat it as you may. So what
is white space? Philosophically speaking, white space is your programming canvas. Misused
it can strain the reader's eyes; painted properly it can be a benefit. A few examples of how
white space can be controlled are with braces and indentation.

Indentation is a must as it guides your eyes in and out of program control. For example,
looking at the following sample `main()` function, your eyes quickly tell you the code inside
the function logically belongs to it.

```
main()
{
  //you code in here
}
```

A common discussion around indentation is the age old argument of tabs versus spaces. This argument can be settled pretty easily in favor of spaces. The rationale behind this favor is based on the fact that tabs can be set to take up various columns. Another programmer opening your code might not have the same number of columns set for her tabs and consequently the formatting will be off.

Another common question with beginning programmers is how far to indent. Personally, I prefer an indentation of two to four spaces. An indentation of longer than four spaces will eventually lead to lines that are too long. The goal here is to maintain a consistent indentation style that keeps the lines of code on the computer screen.

One more thing to consider regarding white space is your brace styles, which are closely tied to your indentation style. Just as with indentation, there are a number of brace styles, though you will likely favor either this one

```
main()
{
  //you code in here
}
```

or this one

```
main(){
  //your code in here
}
```

As with any style the choice is yours, though I recommend balancing a style both comfortable to you as well as consistent with what others are using on your team.

Variable Naming Conventions

The following list contains a minimal number of guidelines you should follow when declaring and naming your variables.

- Identify data types with a prefix.
- Use upper- and lowercase letters appropriately.
- Give variables meaningful names.

There is no one correct way of implementing a nomenclature for your variable names, although some are better than others. After identifying your naming standards, the most important process is to stay consistent with those practices throughout each of your programs.

In the next few sections, I'll show you a couple of different ways that have worked for me and for many other programmers who have used the guidelines in the preceding list.

In addition to adhering to a variable naming convention, be cautious not to use reserved characters in your variable names. As a general rule, abide by the following suggestions:

- Always begin your variable names with a lowercase letter.
- Do not use spaces in your variable names.
- Only use letters, numbers, and underscores (_) in your variable names.
- Keep variable names fewer than 31 characters to maintain ANSI C standards.

Identifying Data Types with a Prefix

When working with variables, I tend to choose one of three types of prefixes, as demonstrated next.

```
int intOperand1;
float fltResult;
char chrMiddleInitial;
```

For each variable data type, I choose a three-character prefix, int (short for integer), flt (short for float), and chr (short for character), for my variable name prefixes. When I see these variables in my program code, I know instantly what data types they are.

Another way of prefixing your integer data types is to use a single-character prefix, as shown in the second variable declarations.

```
int iOperand1;
float fResult;
char cMiddleInitial;
```

Even though these variables don't scream out their data types, you can see their prefix easily when trying to determine variable content type. Also, these single-character prefixes work very well when used in conjunction with appropriate upper- and lowercase letters, as discussed in the next section.

Using Uppercase and Lowercase Letters Appropriately

Capitalizing the first character of each word in a variable name (as shown in the following code) is the most common and preferred variable naming convention.

```
float fNetSalary;
char cMenuSelection;
int iBikeInventoryTotal;
```

Using uppercase characters in each word makes it very easy to read the variable name and identify its purpose. Now, take a look at the same variables with the same name, only this time without using uppercase characters.

```
float fnetsalary;
char cmenuselection;
int ibikeinventorytotal;
```

Which variable names are easier to read?

In addition to using uppercase letters for readability, some programmers like to use the underscore character to break up words, as shown in the following code.

```
float f_Net_Salary;
char c_Menu_Selection;
int i_Bike_Inventory_Total;
```

Using the underscore character certainly creates a readable variable, but it is a bit too cumbersome for me.

Constant data types provide another challenge for creating a standard naming convention. Personally, I like the following naming conventions.

```
const int  constWeeks = 52;
const int  WEEKS = 52;
```

In the first constant declaration I use the `const` prefix for identifying `constWeeks` as a constant. Notice, though, that I still capitalize the first letter in the constant name for readability purposes.

In the second declaration, I simply capitalize every letter in the constant name. This naming style really stands out.

Give Variables Meaningful Names

Giving your variables meaningful names is probably the most important part of variable naming conventions. Doing so creates self-documenting code. Consider the following section of code, which uses comments to describe the variable's purpose.

```
int x; //x is the Age
int y; //y is the Distance
int z; //z is the Result
```

The preceding variable declarations do not use meaningful names and thus require some form of documentation to make your code's purpose understandable. Instead, look at the following self-documenting variable names.

```
int iAge;
int iDistance;
int iResult;
```

scanf()

So far, you have learned how to send output to the computer's screen using the `printf()` function. In this section, you will learn how to receive input from users through the `scanf()` function.

The `scanf()` function is another built in function provided by the standard input output library `<stdio.h>`; it reads standard input from the keyboard and stores it in previously declared variables. It takes two arguments as demonstrated next.

```
scanf("conversion specifier", variable);
```

The conversion specifier argument tells `scanf()` how to convert the incoming data. You can use the same conversion specifiers as discussed in Table 2.2, and shown again as relative to `scanf()` in Table 2.3.

TABLE 2.3 COMMON CONVERSION SPECIFIERS USED WITH SCANF()	
Conversion Specifier	**Description**
%d	Receives integer value
%f	Receives floating-point numbers
%c	Receives character

The following code represents a complete C program, the Adder program, which uses the scanf() function to read in two integers and add them together. Its output is shown in Figure 2.4.

```c
#include <stdio.h>

main()

{

    int iOperand1 = 0;
    int iOperand2 = 0;

    printf("\n\tAdder Program, by Michael Vine\n");
    printf("\nEnter first operand: ");
    scanf("%d", &iOperand1);
    printf("Enter second operand: ");
    scanf("%d", &iOperand2);
    printf("The result is %d\n", iOperand1 + iOperand2);

}
```

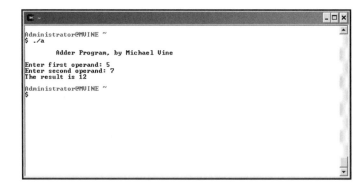

FIGURE 2.4

Using scanf() to receive input from a user.

The first notable line of code prompts the user to enter a number.

```c
printf("\nEnter first operand: ");
```

You may notice that the printf function above does not contain a variable at the end, nor does it include the escape sequence \n at the end of the statement. By leaving the new line escape sequence off the end of a print statement, program control pauses while waiting for user input.

The next line of code uses the `scanf()` function to receive input from the user.

```
scanf("%d", &iOperand1);
```

The first `scanf()` argument takes the integer conversion specifier (`"%d"`), which tells the program to convert the incoming value to an integer. The second operator is an address operator (&), followed by the name of the variable.

Essentially, the address operator contains a pointer to the location in memory where your variable is located. You will learn more about the address operator (&) in Chapter 7, when I discuss pointers. For now, just know that you must precede variable names with it when using the `scanf()` function.

CAUTION   Forgetting to place the address operator (&) in front of your variable in a `scanf()` function will not always generate compile errors, but it will cause problems with memory access during program execution.

After receiving both numbers (operands) from the user, I then use a print statement to display the following result.

```
printf("The result is %d\n", iOperand1 + iOperand2);
```

In this print statement, I include a single conversion specifier (%d), which tells the program to display a single integer value. In the next argument of the `printf()` function, I add both numbers input by the user using the addition sign (+).

ARITHMETIC IN C

As demonstrated in the Adder program from the previous section, C enables programmers to perform all types of arithmetic. Table 2.4 demonstrates the most common arithmetic operators used in beginning C programming.

In the Adder program from the previous section, I used a shortcut when dealing with common arithmetic: I performed my calculation in the `printf()` function. Although this is not required, you can use additional variables and program statements to derive the same outcome. For example, the following code is another variation of the Adder program that uses additional program statements to achieve the same result.

TABLE 2.4		COMMON ARITHMETIC OPERATORS	

Operator	Description	Example
*	Multiplication	fResult I fOperand I * fOperand2;
/	Division	fResult I fOperand I / fOperand2;
%	Modulus (remainder)	fRemainder I fOperand I % fOperand2;
+	Addition	fResult I fOperand I + fOperand2;
—	Subtraction	fResult I fOperand I – fOperand2;

```c
#include <stdio.h>

main()

{

    int iOperand1 = 0;
    int iOperand2 = 0;
    int iResult = 0;

    printf("\n\tAdder Program, by Michael Vine\n");
    printf("\nEnter first operand: ");
    scanf("%d", &iOperand1);
    printf("Enter second operand: ");
    scanf("%d", &iOperand2);

    iResult = iOperand1 + iOperand2;

    printf("The result is %d\n", iResult);

}
```

In this deviation of the Adder program, I used two additional statements to derive the same outcome. Instead of performing the arithmetic in the `printf()` function, I've declared an additional variable called iResult and assigned to it the result of iOperand1 + iOperand2 using a separate statement, as demonstrated next.

```c
iResult = iOperand1 + iOperand2;
```

Remember that the equal sign (=) is an assignment operator, where the right side is being assigned to the left side of the operator (=). For example, you would not say the following:

```
iResult equals iOperand1 plus iOperand2.
```

That is incorrectly stated. Instead you would say:

```
iResult gets the value of iOperand1 plus iOperand2.
```

OPERATOR PRECEDENCE

Operator precedence is very important when dealing with arithmetic in any programming language. Operator precedence in C is shown in Table 2.5.

TABLE 2.5	OPERATOR PRECEDENCE
Order or Precedence	**Description**
( )	Parentheses are evaluated first, from innermost to outermost
*, /, %	Evaluated second, from left to right
+, −	Evaluated last, from left to right

Take the following formula, for example, which uses parentheses to dictate the proper order of operations.

```
f = (a - b)(x - y);
```

Given $a = 5, b = 1, x = 10$, and $y = 5$, you could implement the formula in C using the following syntax.

```
intF = (5 - 1) * (10 - 5);
```

Using the correct order of operations, the value of `intF` would be 20. Take another look at the same implementation in C —this time without using parentheses to dictate the correct order of operations.

```
intF = 5 - 1 * 10 - 5;
```

Neglecting to implement the correct order of operations, `intF` would result in −10.

CHAPTER PROGRAM—PROFIT WIZ

As shown in Figure 2.5, the Profit Wiz program uses many chapter-based concepts, such as variables, input and output with `printf()` and `scanf()` functions, and beginning arithmetic.

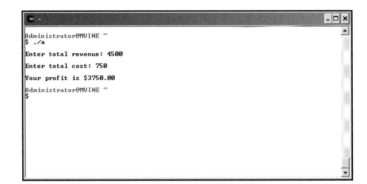

FIGURE 2.5

Demonstrating
chapter-based
concepts with the
Profit Wiz
program.

All of the C code needed to create the Profit Wiz program is demonstrated next.

```c
#include <stdio.h>

main()

{

    float fRevenue, fCost;

    fRevenue = 0;
    fCost = 0;

    /* profit = revenue - cost */

    printf("\nEnter total revenue: ");
    scanf("%f", &fRevenue);
    printf("\nEnter total cost: ");
    scanf("%f", &fCost);
    printf("\nYour profit is $%.2f\n", fRevenue - fCost);

}
```

SUMMARY

- A computer's long-term memory is called *nonvolatile* memory and is generally associated with mass storage devices, such as hard drives, large disk arrays, diskettes, and CD-ROMs.

- A computer's short-term memory is called *volatile* memory, it loses its data when power is removed from the computer.

- Integers are whole numbers that represent positive and negative numbers.

- Floating-point numbers represent all numbers, including signed and unsigned decimal and fractional numbers.

- Signed numbers include positive and negative numbers, whereas unsigned numbers can only include positive values.

- Character data types are representations of integer values known as *character codes.*

- Conversion specifiers are used to display unreadable data in a computer's memory as information.

- Constant data types retain their data values during program execution.

- White space is ignored by compilers and is commonly managed for readability using programming styles such as indentation and brace placement.

- Three useful rules for naming conventions include:

  1. Identify data types with a prefix.
  2. Use upper- and lowercase letters appropriately.
  3. Give variables meaningful names.

- The `scanf()` function reads standard input from the keyboard and stores it in previously declared variables.

- The equal sign (=) is an assignment operator, where the right side of the assignment operator is assigned to the left side of the operator.

- In operator precedence parentheses are evaluated first, from innermost to outermost.

CHALLENGES

1. Given a = 5, b = 1, x = 10, and y = 5, create a program that outputs the result of the formula f = (a − b)(x − y) using a single `printf()` function.

2. Create a program that uses the same formula above to output the result; this time, however, prompt the user for the values a, b, x, and y. Use appropriate variable names and naming conventions.

3. Create a program that prompts a user for her name. Store the user's name using the `scanf()` function and return a greeting back to the user using her name.

4. Create a new program that prompts a user for numbers and determines total revenue using the following formula: `Total Revenue = Price * Quantity`.

5. Build a new program that prompts a user for data and determines a commission using the following formula: `Commission = Rate * (Sales Price - Cost)`.

CONDITIONS

In this chapter I will guide you through the next series of essential programming concepts known as conditions. *Conditions* (often called program control, decisions, or expressions) allow you to make decisions about program direction. Learning how to use and build conditions in your program code will give you a more fluid and interactive program.

Along the way, I will introduce essential beginning computer science theories that will help you learn the fundamental concepts of algorithm analysis and Boolean algebra. Reviewing these topics will provide you with the necessary background for understanding conditional program control.

Specifically, this chapter covers the following topics:

- Algorithms for conditions
- Simple if structure
- Nested if structure
- Boolean algebra
- Compound if structures and input validation
- The switch structure
- Random numbers

ALGORITHMS FOR CONDITIONS

Algorithms are the foundation for computer science. In fact, many computer science professors say that computer science is really the analysis of algorithms.

An algorithm is a finite step-by-step process for solving a problem that begins with a problem statement. It is this problem statement that programmers use to formulate an algorithm for solving the problem. Keep in mind, the process of building algorithms and algorithm analysis occurs before any program code has been written.

To get a visual picture of algorithms, programmers and analysts commonly use one of two tools to demonstrate program flow (the algorithm). In the next few sections, I will show you how to build and use two algorithm tools: pseudo code and flowcharts.

Expressions and Conditional Operators

Conditional operators are a key factor when building and evaluating expressions in pseudo code, flowcharts, or any programming language.

Not all programming languages, however, use the same conditional operators, so it is important to note what operators C uses.

Table 3.1 lists the conditional operators used in C.

TABLE 3.1	CONDITIONAL OPERATORS
Operator	**Description**
==	Equal (two equal signs)
!=	Not equal
>	Greater than
<	Less than
>=	Greater than or equal to
<=	Less than or equal to

When conditional operators are used to build expressions (conditions), the result is either true or false. Table 3.2 demonstrates the true/false results when using conditional operators.

Pseudo Code

Pseudo code is frequently used by programmers to aid in developing algorithms. It is primarily a marriage between human-like language and actual programming language. Because of its

TABLE 3.2 EXPRESSIONS DEMONSTRATED	
Expression	**Result**
5 == 5	True
5 != 5	False
5 > 5	False
5 < 5	False
5 >= 5	True
5 <= 5	True

likeness to programming syntax, it has always been more popular among programmers than analysts.

Because there are many different programming languages with varying syntax, pseudo code can easily vary from one programmer to another. For example, even though two programmers are solving the same problem, a C programmer's pseudo code may look a bit different than a Visual Basic programmer's pseudo code.

Nevertheless, if used appropriately and without heavy dependence on language specifics, pseudo code can be a wonderful and powerful tool for programmers to quickly write down and analyze an algorithm. Take the following problem statement, for example.

Turn the air conditioning on when the temperature is greater than or equal to 80 degrees or else turn it off.

Given this problem statement, my algorithm implemented in pseudo code will look like the following:

```
if temperature >= 80
    Turn AC on
else
    Turn AC off
end if
```

The preceding pseudo code uses a combination of language and programming syntax to depict the flow of the algorithm; however, if inserted into a C program, it would not compile. But that's not the point of pseudo code. Programmers use pseudo code as a shorthand notation for demonstrating what an algorithm looks like, but not necessarily what the program code will look like. Once the pseudo code has been written down you can easily transform pseudo code to any programming language.

How the pseudo code is written is ultimately up to you, but you should always try to keep it as language independent as possible.

Here's another problem statement that requires the use of decision-making.

Allow a customer to deposit or withdraw money from a bank account, and if a user elects to withdraw funds, ensure that sufficient monies exist.

Pseudo code for this problem statement might look like the following.

```
if action == deposit
    Deposit funds into account
else
    if balance < withdraw amount
        Insufficient funds for transaction
    else
        Withdraw monies
    end if
end if
```

The first point of interest in the preceding pseudo code is that I have a nested condition inside a parent condition. This nested condition is said to belong to its parent condition, such that the nested condition will never be evaluated unless one of the parent conditional requirements is met. In this case, the action must not equal the deposit for the nested condition to be evaluated.

Also notice that for each algorithm implemented with pseudo code, I use a standard form of indentation to improve the readability.

Take a look at the same pseudo code; this time without the use of indentation.

```
if action == deposit
Deposit funds into account
else
if balance < withdraw amount
Insufficient funds for transaction
else
Withdraw monies
end if
end if
```

You probably already see the benefit of using indentation for readability as the preceding pseudo code is difficult to read and follow. Without indentation in your pseudo code or actual program code, it is extremely difficult to pinpoint nested conditions.

In the next section, you will learn how to implement the same algorithms, shown previously, with flowcharts.

Flowcharts

Popular among computing analysts, *flowcharts* use graphical symbols to depict an algorithm or program flow. In this section, I'll use four common flowchart symbols to depict program flow, as shown in Figure 3.1.

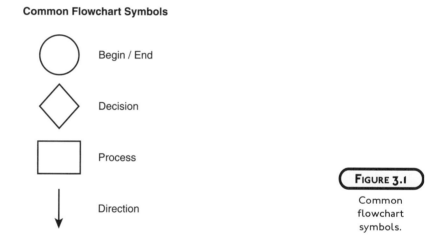

Common Flowchart Symbols

Begin / End

Decision

Process

Direction

FIGURE 3.1

Common flowchart symbols.

To demonstrate flowchart techniques, take another look at the AC algorithm used in the previous section.

```
if temperature >= 80
    Turn AC on
else
    Turn AC off
end if
```

This AC algorithm can also be easily represented using flowchart techniques, as shown in Figure 3.2.

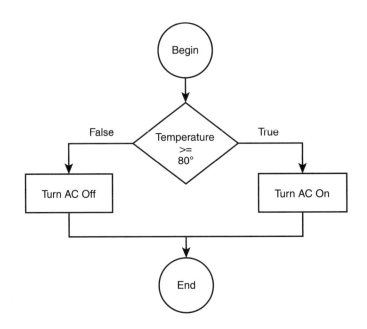

FIGURE 3.2

Flowchart for the
AC algorithm.

The flowchart in Figure 3.2 uses a decision symbol to illustrate an expression. If the expression evaluates to `true`, program flow moves to the right, processes a statement, and then terminates. If the expression evaluates to `false`, program flow moves to the left, processes a different statement, and then terminates.

As a general rule of thumb, your flowchart's decision symbols should always move to the right when an expression evaluates to `true`. However, there are times when you will not care if an expression evaluates to `false`. For example, take a look at the following algorithm implemented in pseudo code.

```
if target hit == true
   Incrementing player's score
end if
```

In the preceding pseudo code, I'm only concerned about incrementing the player's score when a target has been hit. I could demonstrate the same algorithm using a flowchart, as shown in Figure 3.3.

You can still use flowcharts to depict more complicated decisions, such as nested conditions, but you must pay closer attention to program flow. To demonstrate, take another look at the pseudo code used earlier to depict a sample banking process.

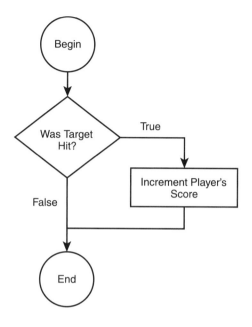

FIGURE 3.3

Flowchart for the
target hit
algorithm.

```
if action == deposit
   Deposit funds into account
else
   if balance < withdraw amount
      insufficient funds for transaction
   else
      Withdraw monies
   end if
end if
```

The flowchart version of this algorithm is shown in Figure 3.4.

You can see in Figure 3.4 that I've used two diamond symbols to depict two separate decisions. But how do you know which diamond represents a nested condition? Good question. When looking at flowcharts, it can be difficult to see nested conditions at first, but remember that anything (process or condition) after the first diamond symbol (condition) actually belongs to that condition and therefore is nested inside it.

In the next few sections, I'll go from theory to application and discuss how to use C's if structure to implement simple, nested, and compound conditions.

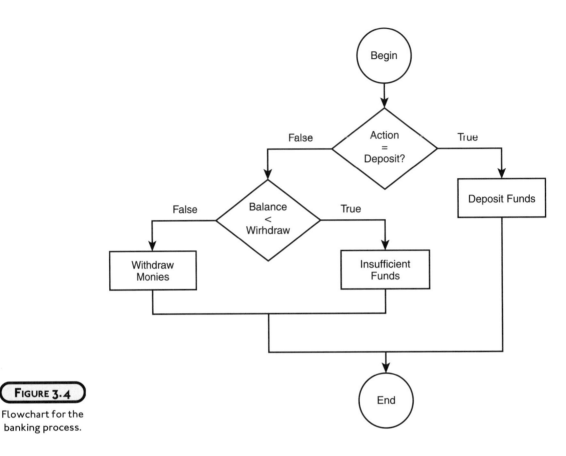

FIGURE 3.4

Flowchart for the
banking process.

SIMPLE IF STRUCTURES

As you will see shortly, the if structure in C is similar to the pseudo code discussed earlier, with a few minor exceptions. To demonstrate, take another look at the AC algorithm in pseudo code form.

```
if temperature >= 80
    Turn AC on
else
    Turn AC off
end if
```

The preceding pseudo code is implemented in C, as demonstrated next.

```
if (iTemperature >= 80)
    //Turn AC on
else
    //Turn AC off
```

The first statement is the condition, which checks for a true or false result in the expression (iTemperature >= 80). The expression must be enclosed in parentheses. If the expression's result is true, the Turn AC on code is executed; if the expression's result is false, the else part of the condition is executed. Also note that there is no end if statement in C.

If you process more than one statement inside your conditions, you must enclose the multiple statements in braces, as shown next.

```
if (iTemperature >= 80) {
    //Turn AC on
    printf("\nThe AC is on\n");
}
else {
    //Turn AC off
    printf("\nThe AC is off\n");
}
```

The placement of each brace is only important in that they begin and end the statement blocks. For example, I can change the placement of braces in the preceding code without affecting the outcome, as demonstrated next.

```
if (ITemperature >= 80)
{
    //Turn AC on
    printf("\nThe AC is on\n");
}
else
{
    //Turn AC off
    printf("\nThe AC is off\n");
}
```

Essentially, consistency is the most important factor here. Simply choose a style of brace placement that works for you and stick with it.

From abstract to implementation, take a look at Figure 3.5, which uses basic if structures to implement a small program.

FIGURE 3.5

Demonstrating
basic if
structures.

All the code needed to implement Figure 3.5 is shown next.

```c
#include <stdio.h>

main()
{

    int iResponse = 0;

    printf("\n\tAC Control Unit\n");
    printf("\n1\tTurn the AC on\n");
    printf("2\tTurn the AC off\n");
    printf("\nEnter your selection: ");
    scanf("%d", &iResponse);

    if (iResponse == 1)
        printf("\nAC is now on\n");

    if (iResponse == 2)
        printf("\nAC is now off\n");

}
```

Reviewing the code, I use the printf() functions to first display a menu system. Next, I use the scanf() function to receive the user's selection and finally I compare the user's input (using if structures) against two separate valid numbers. Depending on the conditions' results, I output a message to the user.

Notice in my if structure that I'm comparing an integer variable to a number. This is acceptable—you can use variables in your if structures as long as you are comparing apples to apples and oranges to oranges. In other words, you can use a combination of variables and other data in your expressions as long as you're comparing numbers to numbers and characters to characters.

To demonstrate, here's the same program code again, this time using characters as menu choices.

```
#include <stdio.h>

main()
{

    char cResponse = '\0';

    printf("\n\tAC Control Unit\n");
    printf("\na\tTurn the AC on\n");
    printf("b\tTurn the AC off\n");
    printf("\nEnter your selection: ");
    scanf("%c", &cResponse);

    if (cResponse == 'a')
        printf("\nAC is now on\n");

    if (cResponse == 'b')
        printf("\nAC is now off\n");

}
```

I changed my variable from an integer data type to a character data type and modified my scanf() function and if structures to accommodate the use of a character-based menu.

NESTED IF STRUCTURES

Take another look at the banking process implemented in pseudo code to demonstrate nested if structures in C.

```
if action == deposit
    Deposit funds into account
else
```

```
    if balance < withdraw amount
        Insufficient funds for transaction
    else
        Withdraw monies
    end if
end if
```

Because there are multiple statements inside the parent condition's else clause, I will need to use braces when implementing the algorithm in C (shown next).

```c
if (action == deposit) {
    //deposit funds into account
    printf("\nFunds deposited\n");
}
else {
    if (balance < withdraw)
        //insufficient funds
    else
        //withdraw monies
}
```

To implement the simple banking system, I made the minor assumption that the customer's account already contains a balance. To assume this, I hard coded the initial balance into the variable declaration as the following code demonstrates. Sample output from the banking system can be seen in Figure 3.6.

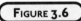

FIGURE 3.6

Demonstrating nested if structures with banking system rules.

```c
#include <stdio.h>

main()
{

    int iSelection = 0;
    float fTransAmount = 0.0;
    float fBalance = 100.25;

    printf("\n\tATM\n");
    printf("\n1\tDeposit Funds\n");
    printf("2\tWithdraw Funds\n");
    printf("\nEnter your selection: ");
    scanf("%d", &iSelection);

    if (iSelection == 1) {
        printf("\nEnter fund amount to deposit: ");
        scanf("%f", &fTransAmount);
        printf("\nYour new balance is: $%.2f\n", fBalance + fTransAmount);
    } //end if

    if (iSelection == 2) {
        printf("\nEnter fund amount to withdraw: ");
        scanf("%f", &fTransAmount);

        if (fTransAmount > fBalance)
            printf("\nInsufficient funds\n");
        else
            printf("\nYour new balance is $%.2f\n", fBalance - fTransAmount);

    } //end if

} //end main function
```

Notice my use of comments when working with the if structures to denote the end of logical blocks. Essentially, I do this to minimize confusion about the purpose of many ending braces, which can litter even a simple program.

INTRODUCTION TO BOOLEAN ALGEBRA

Before I discuss the next type of conditions, compound `if` structures, I want to give you some background on compound conditions using Boolean algebra.

BOOLEAN ALGEBRA

Boolean algebra is named after George Boole, a mathematician in the nineteenth century. Boole developed his own branch of logic containing the values `true` and `false` and the operators `and`, `or`, and `not` to manipulate the values.

Even though Boole's work was before the advent of computers, his research has become the foundation of today's modern digital circuitry in computer architecture.

As the subsequent sections will discuss, Boolean algebra commonly uses three operators (`and`, `or`, and `not`) to manipulate two values (`true` and `false`).

and Operator

The `and` operator is used to build compound conditions. Each side of the condition must be `true` for the entire condition to be `true`. Take the following expression, for example.

```
3 == 3 and 4 == 4
```

This compound condition contains two separate expressions or conditions, one on each side of the `and` operator. The first condition evaluates to `true` and so does the second condition, which generates a `true` result for the entire expression.

Here's another compound condition that evaluates to `false`.

```
3==4 and 4==4
```

This compound condition evaluates to `false` because one side of the `and` operator does not evaluate to `true`. Study Table 3.3 to get a better picture of possible outcomes with the `and` operator.

Truth tables allow you to see all possible scenarios in an expression containing compound conditions. The truth table in Table 3.3 shows two possible input values (x and y) for the `and` operator. As you can see, there is only one possible combination for the `and` operator to generate a `true` result: when both sides of the condition are `true`.

TABLE 3.3 TRUTH TABLE FOR THE AND OPERATOR		
x	**y**	**Result**
true	true	true
true	false	false
false	true	false
false	false	false

or Operator

The or operator is similar to the and operator in that it contains at least two separate expressions and is used to build a compound condition. The or operator, however, differs in that it only requires one side of the compound condition to be true for the entire expression to be true. Take the following compound condition, for example.

```
4 == 3 or 4 == 4
```

In the compound condition above, one side evaluates to false and the other to true, providing a true result for the entire expression. To demonstrate all possible scenarios for the or operator, study the truth table in Table 3.4.

TABLE 3.4 TRUTH TABLE FOR THE OR OPERATOR		
x	**y**	**Result**
true	true	true
true	false	true
false	true	true
false	false	false

Notice that Table 3.4 depicts only one scenario when the or operator generates a false outcome: when both sides of the operator result in false values.

not Operator

The last Boolean operator I discuss in this chapter is the not operator. The not operator is easily understood at first, but can certainly be a bit confusing when programmed in compound conditions.

Essentially, the not operator generates the opposite value of whatever the current result is. For example, the following expression uses the not operator in a compound condition.

```
not( 4 == 4 )
```

The inside expression, 4 == 4, evaluates to true, but the not operator forces the entire expression to result in false. In other words, the opposite of true is false.

Take a look at Table 3.5 to evaluate the not operator further.

TABLE 3.5 TRUTH TABLE FOR THE NOT OPERATOR	
x	**Result**
true	false
false	true

Notice that the not operator contains only one input variable (x) to build a compound condition.

 C evaluates all non-zero values as true and all zero values as false.

Order of Operations

Now that you've seen how the Boolean operators and, or, and not work, you can further your problem-solving skills with Boolean algebra. Before you take that plunge, however, I must discuss order of operations for a moment.

Order of operations becomes extremely important when dealing with compound conditions in Boolean algebra or with implementation in any programming language.

To dictate order of operations, use parentheses to build clarification into your compound conditions. For example, given x = 1, y = 2, and z = 3, study the following compound condition.

```
z < y or z <= z and x < z
```

Without using parentheses to dictate order of operations, you must assume that the order of operations for the compound condition flows from left to right. To see how this works, I've broken down the problem in the following example:

1. First, the expression `z < y or z <= z` is executed, which results in `false or true`, and results in the overall result of `true`.
2. Next, the expression `true and x < z` is executed, which results in `true and true`, and results in the overall value of `true`.

But when I change the order of operations using parentheses, I get a different overall result as shown next.

```
z < y or (z < x and x < z)
```

1. First, `(z < x and x < z)` is evaluated, which results in `false and true`, and results in the overall value of `false`.
2. Next, the expression `z < y or false` is evaluated, which results in `false or false`, and results in the overall value of `false`.

You should now see the consequence of using or not using parentheses to guide the order of operations.

Building Compound Conditions with Boolean Operators

Using Boolean operators and order of operations, you can easily build and solve Boolean algebra problems. Practicing this type of problem solving will certainly strengthen your analytic abilities, which will ultimately make you a stronger programmer when incorporating compound conditions into your programs.

Try to solve the following Boolean algebra problems, given

```
x == 5, y == 3, and z == 4
```

1. `x > 3 and z == 4`
2. `y >= 3 or z > 4`
3. `NOT(x == 4 or y < z)`
4. `(z == 5 or x > 3) and (y == z or x < 10)`

Table 3.6 lists the answers for the preceding Boolean algebra problems.

TABLE 3.6	ANSWERS TO BOOLEAN ALGEBRA PROBLEMS
Question	**Answer**
1	true
2	true
3	false
4	true

COMPOUND IF STRUCTURES AND INPUT VALIDATION

You can use your newly learned knowledge of compound conditions to build compound if conditions in C, or any other programming language for that matter.

Like Boolean algebra, compound if conditions in C commonly use the operators and and or, as demonstrated in Table 3.7.

TABLE 3.7	COMMON CHARACTER SETS USED TO IMPLEMENT COMPOUND CONDITIONS	
Character Set	**Boolean Operator**
&&	and
||	or

As you will see in the next few sections, these character sets can be used in various expressions to build compound conditions in C.

&& Operator

The && operator implements the Boolean operator and; it uses two ampersands to evaluate a Boolean expression from left to right. Both sides of the operator must evaluate to true before the entire expression becomes true.

The following two code blocks demonstrate C's && operator in use. The first block of code uses the and operator (&&) in a compound if condition, which results in a true expression.

```
if ( 3 > 1 && 5 < 10 )
    printf("The entire expression is true\n");
```

The next compound if condition results in false.

```
if ( 3 > 5 && 5 < 5 )
    printf("The entire expression is false\n");
```

|| Operator

The || character set (or Boolean operator) uses two pipe characters to form a compound condition, which is also evaluated from left to right. If either side of the condition is true, the whole expression results in true.

The following code block demonstrates a compound if condition using the || operator, which results in a true expression.

```
if ( 3 > 5 || 5 <= 5 )
    printf("The entire expression is true\n");
```

The next compound condition evaluates to false because neither side of the || operator evaluates to true.

```
if ( 3 > 5 || 6 < 5 )
    printf("The entire expression is false\n");
```

 Consider using braces around a single statement in an if condition. For example, the following program code

```
if ( 3 > 5 || 6 < 5 )
    printf("The entire expression is false\n");
```

Is the same as

```
if ( 3 > 5 || 6 < 5 ) {
    printf("The entire expression is false\n");
}
```

The if condition that uses braces around the single line statement helps to ensure that all subsequent modifications to the if statement remain logic-error free. Lots of logic errors creep into code when programmers begin adding statements to single line if bodies and forget to add the braces, which THEN are required.

Checking for Upper- and Lowercase

You may remember from Chapter 2, "Primary Data Types," that characters are represented by ASCII character sets, such that letter a is represented by ASCII character set 97 and letter A is represented by ASCII character set 65.

So what does this mean to you or me? Take the following C program, for example.

```
 #include <stdio.h>

main()
{

    char cResponse = '\0';
```

```
   printf("Enter the letter A: ");
   scanf("%c", &cResponse);

   if ( cResponse == 'A' )
      printf("\nCorrect response\n");
   else
      printf("\nIncorrect response\n");

}
```

In the preceding program, what response would you get after entering the letter a? You may guess that you would receive Incorrect response. This is because the ASCII value for uppercase letter A is not the same as the ASCII value for lowercase letter a. (To see a listing of common ASCII characters, visit Appendix D, "Common ASCII Character Codes.")

To build user-friendly programs, you should use compound conditions to check for both upper- and lowercase letters, as shown in the following modified if condition.

```
if ( cResponse == 'A' || cResponse == 'a' )
```

To build a complete and working compound condition, you must have two separate and valid conditions on each side of the operator. A common mistake among beginning programmers is to build an invalid expression on one or more of the operator's sides. The following compound conditions are not valid.

```
if ( cResponse == 'A' || 'a' )

if ( cResponse == 'A' || == 'a' )

if ( cResponse || cResponse )
```

None of the expressions is complete on both sides, and, therefore, the expressions are incorrectly built. Take another look at the correct version of this compound condition, shown next.

```
if ( cResponse == 'A' || cResponse == 'a' )
```

Checking for a Range of Values

Checking for a range of values is a common programming practice for input validation. You can use compound conditions and relational operators to check for value ranges, as shown in the following program:

```
#include <stdio.h>

main()
{

    int iResponse = 0;

    printf("Enter a number from 1 to 10: ");
    scanf("%d", &iResponse);

    if ( iResponse < 1 || iResponse > 10 )
        printf("\nNumber not in range\n");
    else
        printf("\nThank you\n");

}
```

The main construct of this program is the compound if condition. This compound expression uses the || (or) operator to evaluate two separate conditions. If either of the conditions results in true, I know that the user has entered a number that is not between one and 10.

isdigit() Function

The isdigit() function is part of the character-handling library <ctype.h> and is a wonderful tool for aiding you in validating user input. Specifically, the isdigit() function can be used to verify that the user has entered either digits or non-digit characters. Moreover, the isdigit() function returns true if its passed-in value evaluates to a digit, and false (0) if not.

As shown next, the isdigit() function takes one parameter.

```
isdigit(x)
```

If the parameter x is a digit, the isdigit() function will return a true value; otherwise, a 0 or false will be sent back to the calling expression.

Remember to include the <ctype.h> library in your program when using the isdigit() function, as demonstrated next.

```
#include <stdio.h>
#include <ctype.h>

main()
```

```
{

    char cResponse = '\0';

    printf("\nPlease enter a letter: ");
    scanf("%c", &cResponse);

    if ( isdigit(cResponse) == 0 )
       printf("\nThank you\n");
    else
       printf("\nYou did not enter a letter\n");

}
```

This program uses the isdigit() function to verify that the user has entered a letter or non-digit. If the user enters, for example, the letter a, the isdigit() returns a zero (false). But if the user enters the number 7, then isdigit() returns a true value.

Essentially, the preceding program uses the isdigit() function a bit backward to verify non-digit data. Take a look at the next program, which uses isdigit() in a more conventional manner.

```
#include <stdio.h>
#include <ctype.h>

main()
{

    char cResponse = '\0';


    printf("\nPlease enter a digit: ");
    scanf("%c", &cResponse);

    if isdigit(cResponse)
       printf("\nThank you\n");
    else
       printf("\nYou did not enter a digit\n");

}
```

Notice that I did not evaluate the `isdigit()` function to anything in the preceding `if` condition. This means that I do not need to surround my expression in parentheses.

You can do this in any `if` condition, as long as the expression or function returns a `true` or `false` (Boolean) value. In this case, `isdigit()` does return `true` or `false`, which is sufficient for the C `if` condition. For example, if the user enters a 7, which I pass to `isdigit()`—`isdigit()` returns a `true` value that satisfies the condition.

Take another look at the condition part of the preceding program to ensure that you grasp this concept.

```
if isdigit(cResponse)
  printf("\nThank you\n");
else
  printf("\nYou did not enter a digit\n");
```

THE SWITCH STRUCTURE

The `switch` structure is another common language block used to evaluate conditions. It is most commonly implemented when programmers have a specific set of choices they are evaluating from a user's response, much like a menu. The following sample code demonstrates how the `switch` structure is built.

```
switch (x) {

    case 1:
        //x Is 1
    case 2:
        //x Is 2
    case 3:
        //x Is 3
    case 4:
        //x Is 4


}  //end switch
```

Note that the preceding `switch` structure requires the use of braces.

In this example, the variable x is evaluated in each `case` structure following the `switch` statement. But, how many `case` statements must you use? Simply answered, the number of `case` statements you decide to use depends on how many possibilities your `switch` variable contains.

For example, the following program uses the switch structure to evaluate a user's response from a menu.

```c
#include <stdio.h>

main()
{

    int iResponse = 0;


    printf("\n1\tSports\n");
    printf("2\tGeography\n");
    printf("3\tMusic\n");
    printf("4\tWorld Events\n");
    printf("\nPlease select a category (1-4): ");
    scanf("%d", &iResponse);

    switch (iResponse) {

        case 1:
            printf("\nYou selected sports questions\n");
        case 2:
            printf("You selected geography questions\n");
        case 3:
            printf("You selected music questions\n");
        case 4:
            printf("You selected world event questions\n");

    }  //end switch

}  //end main function
```

Notice the output of the program when I select category 1, as shown in Figure 3.7.

What's wrong with this program's output? When I selected category 1, I should have only been given one response—not four. This bug occurred because after the appropriate case statement is matched to the switch variable, the switch structure continues processing each case statement thereafter.

FIGURE 3.7

Demonstrating
the switch
structure.

This problem is easily solved with the break keyword, as demonstrated next.

```
switch (iResponse) {

    case 1:
        printf("\nYou selected sports questions\n");
        break;
    case 2:
        printf("You selected geography questions\n");
        break;
    case 3:
        printf("You selected music questions\n");
        break;
    case 4:
        printf("You selected world event questions\n");
        break;

} //end switch
```

When C encounters a break statement inside a case block, it stops evaluating any further case statements.

The switch structure also comes with a default block, which can be used to catch any input that does not match the case statements. The following code block demonstrates the default switch section.

```
switch (iResponse) {

    case 1:
```

```
    printf("\nYou selected sports questions\n");
    break;
  case 2:
    printf("You selected geography questions\n");
    break;
  case 3:
    printf("You selected music questions\n");
    break;
  case 4:
    printf("You selected world event questions\n");
    break;
  default:
    printf("Invalid category\n");

} //end switch
```

In addition to evaluating numbers, the switch structure is also popular when choosing between other characters, such as letters. Moreover, you can evaluate like data with multiple case structures on a single line, as shown next.

```
switch (cResponse) {

  case 'a':  case 'A':
    printf("\nYou selected the character a or A\n");
    break;
  case 'b':  case 'B':
    printf("You selected the character b or B\n");
    break;
  case 'c':  case 'C'
    printf("You selected the character c or C\n");
    break;

} //end switch
```

Random Numbers

The concept and application of random numbers can be observed in all types of systems, from encryption programs to games. Fortunately for you and me, the C standard library offers built-in functions for easily generating random numbers. Most notable is the rand() function, which generates a whole number from 0 to a library-defined number, generally at least 32,767.

To generate a specific random set of numbers, say between 1 and 6 (the sides of a die, for example), you will need to define a formula using the rand() function, as demonstrated next.

```
iRandom = (rand() % 6) + 1
```

Starting from the right side of the expression, I use the modulus operator (%) in conjunction with the integer 6 to generate seemingly random numbers between 0 and 5.

Remember that the rand() function generates random numbers starting with 0. To offset this fact, I simply add 1 to the outcome, which increments my random number range from 0 to 5 to 1 to 6. After a random number is generated, I assign it to the iRandom variable.

Here's another example of the rand() function implemented in a complete C program that prompts a user to guess a number from 1 to 10.

```c
#include <stdio.h>

main()
{

    int iRandomNum = 0;
    int iResponse = 0;

    iRandomNum = (rand() % 10) + 1;

    printf("\nGuess a number between 1 and 10: ");
    scanf("%d", &iResponse);

    if (iResponse == iRandomNum)
        printf("\nYou guessed right\n");
    else {
        printf("\nSorry, you guessed wrong\n");
        printf("The correct guess was %d\n", iRandomNum);
    }

}
```

The only problem with this program, and the rand() function for that matter, is that the rand() function generates the same sequence of random numbers repeatedly. Unfortunately, after a user runs the program a few times, he begins to figure out that the same number is generated without randomization.

To correct this, use the srand() function, which produces a true randomization of numbers. More specifically, the srand() function tells the rand() function to produce a true random number every time it is executed.

The srand() function takes an integer number as its starting point for randomizing. To give your program a true sense of randomizing, pass the current time to the srand() function as shown next.

```
srand(time());
```

The time() function returns the current time in seconds, which is a perfect random integer number for the srand() function.

The srand() function only needs to be executed once in your program for it to perform randomization. In the preceding program, I would place the srand() function after my variable declarations but before the rand() function, as demonstrated next.

```
#include <stdio.h>

main()
{

    int iRandomNum = 0;
    int iResponse = 0;
    srand(time());

    iRandomNum = (rand() % 10) + 1;
```

CHAPTER PROGRAM—FORTUNE COOKIE

The Fortune Cookie program (shown in Figure 3.8) uses chapter-based concepts to build a small yet entertaining program that simulates an actual fortune found inside a fortune cookie. To build this program, I used the switch structure and random number generation.

After reading this chapter and with some practice, you should be able to easily follow the Fortune Cookie program code and logic as shown in its entirety next.

FIGURE 3.8

The Fortune
Cookie program.

```c
#include <stdio.h>

main()
{

    int iRandomNum = 0;
    srand(time());

    iRandomNum = (rand() % 4) + 1;

    printf("\nFortune Cookie - Chapter 3\n");

    switch (iRandomNum) {

      case 1:
        printf("\nYou will meet a new friend today.\n");
        break;
      case 2:
        printf("\nYou will enjoy a long and happy life.\n");
        break;
      case 3:
        printf("\nOpportunity knocks softly. Can you hear it?\n");
        break;
      case 4:
        printf("\nYou'll be financially rewarded for your good deeds.\n");
        break;
```

```
} //end switch

printf("\nLucky lotto numbers: ");
printf("%d ", (rand() % 49) + 1);
printf("%d ", (rand() % 49) + 1);
printf("%d ", (rand() % 49) + 1);
printf("%d ", (rand() % 49) + 1);
printf("%d ", (rand() % 49) + 1);
printf("%d\n", (rand() % 49) + 1);

} //end main function
```

SUMMARY

- When conditional operators are used to build expressions, the result is either `true` or `false`.
- Pseudo code is primarily a mix between human-like language and actual programming language and is frequently used by programmers to aid in developing algorithms.
- Flowcharts use graphical symbols to depict an algorithm or program flow.
- Conditions are implemented using the `if` structure, which contains an expression enclosed within parentheses.
- Boolean algebra commonly uses three operators (`and`, `or`, and `not`) to manipulate two values (`true` and `false`).
- Parentheses are used to dictate order of operations and build clarification into compound conditions.
- The `isdigit()` function can be used to verify that the user has entered either digits or non-digit characters.
- The `switch` structure is used to evaluate conditions and is most commonly implemented when a specific set of choices requires evaluation.
- The `rand()` function generates a whole number from 0 to a library-defined number, generally at least 32,767.
- The `srand()` function tells the `rand()` function to produce a true random number every time it is executed.
- The `time()` function returns the current time in seconds, which is a perfect random integer number for the `srand()` function.

CHALLENGES

1. Build a number guessing game that uses input validation (isdigit() function) to verify that the user has entered a digit and not a non-digit (letter). Store a random number between 1 and 10 into a variable each time the program is run. Prompt the user to guess a number between 1 and 10 and alert the user if he was correct or not.

2. Build a Fortune Cookie program that uses either the Chinese Zodiac or astrological signs to generate a fortune, a prediction, or a horoscope based on the user's input. More specifically, the user may need to input her year of birth, month of birth, and day of birth depending on zodiac or astrological techniques used. With this information, generate a custom message or fortune. You can use the Internet to find more information on the Chinese Zodiac or astrology.

3. Create a dice game that uses two six-sided dice. Each time the program runs, use random numbers to assign values to each die variable. Output a "player wins" message to the user if the sum of the two dice is 7 or 11. Otherwise output the sum of the two dice and thank the user for playing.

LOOPING STRUCTURES

n this chapter, I will discuss key programming constructs and techniques for building iteration into your C programs. So what is iteration? Well, *iteration* is a fancy term for loops or looping, or in other words, it's how you build repetition into your programs.

After reading this chapter, you will know how looping structures use conditions to evaluate the number of times a loop should occur. Moreover, you will learn the basic theory and design principals behind looping algorithms using pseudo code and flowcharting techniques. You will also learn new techniques for assigning data and manipulating loops.

This chapter specifically covers the following topics:

- Pseudo code for looping structures
- Flowcharts for looping structures
- Operators continued
- The while loop
- The do while loop
- The for loop
- break and continue statements
- System calls

PSEUDO CODE FOR LOOPING STRUCTURES

Before I discuss the application of iteration, I'll show you some simple theory behind loops using basic algorithm techniques with pseudo code.

Looking back to Chapter 3, "Conditions," you learned that programmers express programming algorithms and key constructs using a combination of human-like language and programming syntax called pseudo code. As demonstrated in this section, pseudo code can also be used to express algorithms for looping structures.

A number of situations require the use of looping techniques, also known as iteration. For example:

- Displaying an ATM (Automated Teller Machine) menu
- Playing a game until the game is over
- Processing employee payroll data until the last employee is read
- Calculating an amortization schedule for a loan
- Keeping the air conditioning on until desired temperature is met
- Maintaining autopilot status until a flight-crew turns it off

To demonstrate looping structures using pseudo code, I'll use processing employee payroll data as an example.

```
while end-of-file == false
    process employee payroll
loop
```

In this pseudo code, I first use a condition to evaluate whether the end of file has been read. If that condition is false (not end of file), I will process employee data. In other words, I will process the payroll until the end of file is true.

The condition in this loop may not be apparent at first, but it's similar to the conditions you learned in Chapter 3. Essentially, the condition in my sample above contains the following expression, which can only result in one of two values, true or false.

```
end-of-file == false
```

At this point, you should notice a recurring theme between conditions and loops. The theme is simple: it's all about conditions! Both looping structures and conditions, such as the if condition and switch structure, use conditional expressions to evaluate whether something happens.

Now take a look at the following pseudo code example that loops through a theoretical payroll file to determine each employee's pay type (salary or hourly).

```
while end-of-file == false
   if pay-type == salary then
      pay = salary
   else
        pay = hours * rate
   end If
loop
```

Sometimes you want the loop's condition at the end, rather than at the beginning. To demonstrate, I can change the location of the loop's condition in the following pseudo code to ensure that a menu is displayed at least once to the end user.

```
do
   display menu
while user-selection != quit
```

By moving the condition to the bottom of the loop, I've guaranteed that the user will have a chance to view the menu at least once.

Loops can contain all kinds of programming statements and structures, including nested conditions and loops. Nested loops provide an interesting study of algorithm analysis because they can be intensive in their process time.

The following block of pseudo code demonstrates the nested loop concept.

```
do
   display menu
   If user-selection == payroll then
      while end-of-file == false
         if pay-type == salary then
            pay = salary
         else
            pay = hours * rate
         end If
      loop
   end if
while user-selection != quit
```

In the preceding pseudo code, I first display a menu. If the user selects to process payroll, I enter a second or inner loop, which processes payroll until the end-of-file has been reached. Once the end-of-file has been reached, the outer loop's condition is evaluated to determine if the user wants to quit. If the user quits, program control is terminated; otherwise, the menu is displayed again.

FLOWCHARTS FOR LOOPING STRUCTURES

Other than those that you learned in Chapter 3, no special symbols are required in flowcharting to represent loops. In fact, you can use the same flowcharting symbols from Chapter 3 to build looping structures in flowcharts.

To demonstrate loops in flowcharts, I'll use the pseudo code from the previous section, "Pseudo Code for Looping Structures." Specifically, I'll build a simple looping structure using a flowchart with the following pseudo code. The resulting flowchart is shown in Figure 4.1.

```
while end-of-file == false
    process employee payroll
loop
```

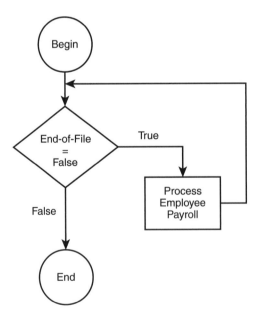

FIGURE 4.1

Flowchart demonstrating a simple looping structure.

In Figure 4.1, I use the diamond symbol to represent a loop. You might be wondering how to tell the difference between the diamond symbols that are used with conditions and loops in a flowchart. Figure 4.1 holds the answer. You can differentiate between conditions and loops in flowcharts by looking at the program flow. If you see connector lines that loop back to the beginning of a condition (diamond symbol), you know that the condition represents a loop. In this example, the program flow moves in a circular pattern. If the condition is true, employee payroll is processed and program control moves back to the beginning of the original condition. Only if the condition is false does the program flow terminate.

Take a look at the next set of pseudo code, which is implemented as a flowchart in Figure 4.2.

```
while end-of-file == false
    if pay-type == salary then
        pay = salary
    else
            pay = hours * rate
    end If
loop
```

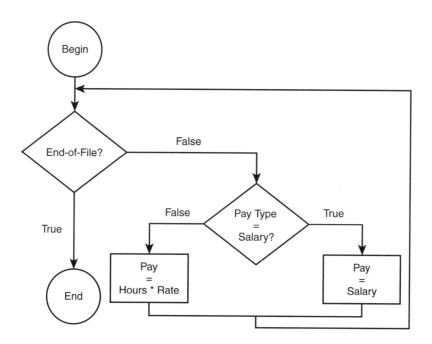

FIGURE 4.2

Flowchart demonstrating a looping structure with inner condition.

In Figure 4.2, you see that the first diamond symbol is really a loop's condition because program flow loops back to its beginning. Inside of the loop, however, is another diamond, which is not a loop. (The inner diamond does not contain program control that loops back to its origin.) Rather, the inner diamond's program flow moves back to the loop's condition regardless of its outcome.

Let's take another look at a previous pseudo code example (the flowchart is shown in Figure 4.3), which moves the condition to the end of the loop.

```
do
    display menu
while user-selection != quit
```

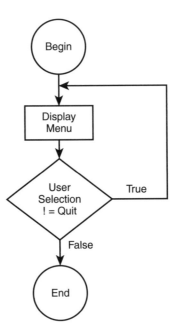

FIGURE 4.3

Moving a loop's condition to the end of the loop.

Remember: The program flow holds the key. Because the loop's condition in Figure 4.3 is at the end of the loop, the first process in the flowchart is displaying the menu. After displaying the menu, the loop's condition is encountered and evaluated. If the loop's condition is true, the program flow loops back to the first process; if false, the program flow terminates.

The final component to building looping algorithms with flowcharts is demonstrating nested loops. Take another look at the nested loop pseudo code from the previous section.

```
do
    display menu
    If user-selection == payroll then
        while end-of-file != true
            if pay-type == salary then
                pay = salary
            else
```

```
        pay = hours * rate
      end If
    loop
  end if
while user-selection != quit
```

Figure 4.4 implements the preceding looping algorithm with flowcharting symbols and techniques.

FIGURE 4.4

Using a flowchart to demonstrate nested loops.

Although Figure 4.4 is much more difficult to follow than the previous flowchart examples, you should still be able to identify the outer and inner (nested) loops by finding the diamonds that have program flow looping back their condition. Out of the four diamonds in Figure 4.4, can you find the two that are loops? Again, to determine which diamond symbol represents a loop, simply identify each diamond that has program control returning to the top part of the diamond.

Here are the two loops in Figure 4.4 represented in pseudo code:

- *while end-of-file != false*
- *while user-selection != quit*

OPERATORS CONTINUED

You've already learned how to assign data to variables using the assignment operator (equal sign). In this section, I'll discuss operators for incrementing and decrementing number-based variables, and I'll introduce new operators for assigning data to variables.

++ Operator

The ++ operator is useful for incrementing number-based variables by 1. To use the ++ operator, simply put it next to a variable, as shown next.

```
iNumberOfPlayers++;
```

To demonstrate further, study the following block of code, which uses the ++ operator to produce the output shown in Figure 4.5.

```
#include <stdio.h>

main()
{
    int x = 0;
    printf("\nThe value of x is %d\n", x);
    x++;
    printf("\nThe value of x is %d\n", x);
}
```

FIGURE 4.5

Incrementing number-based variables by 1 with the ++ operator.

```
Administrator@MVINE ~
$ ./a

The value of x is 0

The value of x is 1

Administrator@MVINE ~
$ 
```

The increment operator (++) can be used in two ways: As demonstrated earlier, you can place the increment operator to the right of a variable, as shown next.

```
x++;
```

This expression tells C to use the current value of variable x and increment it by 1. The variable's original value was 0 (that's what I initialized it to) and 1 was added to 0, which resulted in 1.

The other way to use the increment operator is to place it in front or to the left of your variable, as demonstrated next.

```
++x;
```

Changing the increment operator's placement (postfix versus prefix) with respect to the variable produces different results when evaluated. When the increment operator is placed to the left of the variable, it will increment the variable's contents by 1 first, before it's used in another expression. To get a clearer picture of operator placement, study the following code, which generates the output shown in Figure 4.6.

```
#include <stdio.h>

main()
{

    int x = 0;
    int y = 0;

    printf("\nThe value of y is %d\n", y++);
    printf("\nThe value of x is %d\n", ++x);

}
```

In the first `printf()` function above, C processed the `printf()`'s output first and then incremented the variable y. In the second statement, C increments the x variable first and then processes the `printf()` function, thus revealing the variable's new value. This still may be a bit confusing, so study the next program, which demonstrates increment operator placement further.

```
#include <stdio.h>

main()
```

```
{

    int x = 0;
    int y = 1;

    x = y++ * 2;     //increments x after the assignment
    printf("\nThe value of x is: %d\n", x);

    x = 0;
    y = 1;

    x = ++y * 2;     //increments x before the assignment
    printf("The value of x is: %d\n", x);

}   //end main function
```

The program above will produce the following output.

```
The value of x is: 2
The value of x is: 4
```

Even though most, if not all, C compilers will run the preceding code the way you would expect, due to ANSI C compliance the following statement can produce three different results with three different compilers:

```
anyFunction(++x, x, x++);
```

The argument ++x (using an increment prefix) is NOT guaranteed to be done first before the other arguments (x and x++) are processed. In other words, there is no guarantee that each C compiler will process sequential expressions (an expression separated by commas) the same way.

Let's take a look at another example of postfix and prefix using the increment operator not in a sequential expression (C compiler neutral); the output is revealed in Figure 4.7.

```
#include <stdio.h>

main()
{

    int x = 0;
```

```
int y = 0;

x = y++ * 4;

printf("\nThe value of x is %d\n", x);

y = 0; //reset variable value for demonstration purposes

x = ++y * 4;

printf("\nThe value of x is now %d\n", x);

}
```

FIGURE 4.6

Demonstrating prefix and postfix increment operator placement in a sequential expression.

FIGURE 4.7

Demonstrating prefix and postfix increment operator placement outside of a sequential expression (C compiler neutral).

-- Operator

The - - operator is similar to the increment operator (++), but instead of incrementing number-based variables, it decrements them by 1. Also, like the increment operator, the decrement operator can be placed on both sides (prefix and postfix) of the variable, as demonstrated next.

```
--x;
x--;
```

The next block of code uses the decrement operator in two ways to demonstrate how number-based variables can be decremented by 1.

```c
#include <stdio.h>

main()
{

    int x = 1;
    int y = 1;

    x = y-- * 4;

    printf("\nThe value of x is %d\n", x);

    y = 1; //reset variable value for demonstration purposes

    x = --y * 4;

    printf("\nThe value of x is now %d\n", x);

}
```

The placement of the decrement operator in each print statement is shown in the output, as illustrated in Figure 4.8.

FIGURE 4.8

Demonstrating decrement operators in both prefix and postfix format.

+I Operator

In this section you will learn about another operator that increments a variable to a new value plus itself. First, evaluate the following expression that assigns one variable's value to another.

```c
x = y;
```

The preceding assignment uses a single equal sign to allocate the data in the y variable to the x variable. In this case, x does not equal y; rather, x gets y, or x takes on the value of y.

The += operator is also considered an assignment operator. C provides this friendly assignment operator to increment variables in a new way so that a variable is able to take on a new value plus its current value. To demonstrate its usefulness, study the next line of code, which might be used to maintain a running total **without** the implementation of our newly found operator +=.

```
iRunningTotal = iRunningTotal + iNewTotal;
```

Plug in some numbers to ensure you understand what is happening. For example, say the iRunningTotal variable contains the number 100 and the variable iNewTotal contains the number 50. Using the statement above, what would iRunningTotal be after the statement executed?

If you said 150, you are correct.

Our new increment operator (+=) provides a shortcut to solve the same problem. Take another look at the same expression, this time using the += operator.

```
iRunningTotal += iNewTotal;
```

Using this operator allows you to leave out unnecessary code when assigning the contents of a variable to another. It's important to consider order of operations when working with assignment operators. Normal operations such as addition and multiplication have precedence over the increment operator as demonstrated in the next program.

```c
#include <stdio.h>

main()
{

    int x = 1;
    int y = 2;

    x = y * x + 1;    //arithmetic operations performed before assignment
    printf("\nThe value of x is: %d\n", x);

    x = 1;
```

```
    y = 2;

    x += y * x + 1;    //arithmetic operations performed before assignment
    printf("The value of x is: %d\n", x);

}  //end main function
```

Demonstrating order of operations, the program above outputs the following text.

```
The value of x is: 3
The value of x is: 4
```

It may seem a bit awkward at first, but I'm sure you'll eventually find this assignment operator useful and timesaving.

−= Operator

The -= operator works similarly to the += operator, but instead of adding a variable's contents to another variable, it subtracts the contents of the variable on the right-most side of the expression. To demonstrate, study the following statement, which does not use the -= operator.

```
iRunningTotal = iRunningTotal - iNewTotal;
```

You can surmise from this statement that the variable iRunningTotal is having the variable iNewTotal's contents subtracted from it. You can shorten this statement considerably by using the -= operator as demonstrated next.

```
iRunningTotal -= iNewTotal;
```

Demonstrating the -= assignment further is the following program.

```
#include <stdio.h>

main()
{

    int x = 1;
    int y = 2;

    x = y * x + 1;    //arithmetic operations performed before assignment
    printf("\nThe value of x is: %d\n", x);
```

```
    x = 1;
    y = 2;

    x -= y * x + 1;    //arithmetic operations performed before assignment
    printf("The value of x is: %d\n", x);

}   //end main function
```

Using the `-=` assignment operator in the previous program produces the following output.

```
The value of x is: 3
The value of x is: -2
```

THE WHILE LOOP

Like all of the loops discussed in this chapter, the `while` loop structure is used to create iteration (loops) in your programs, as demonstrated in the following program:

```
#include <stdio.h>

main()
{

    int x = 0;

    while ( x < 10 ) {

        printf("The value of x is %d\n", x);
        x++;

    }   //end while loop

}   //end main function
```

The `while` statement is summarized like this:

```
while ( x < 10 ) {
```

The `while` loop uses a condition (in this case x < 10) that evaluates to either `true` or `false`. As long as the condition is `true`, the contents of the loop are executed. Speaking of the loop's contents, the braces must be used to denote the beginning and end of a loop with multiple statements.

TIP The braces for any loop are required only when more than one statement is included in the loop's body. If your `while` loop contains only one statement, no braces are required. To demonstrate, take a look at the following `while` loop, which does not require the use of braces.

```
while ( x < 10 )
    printf("The value of x is %d\n", x++);
```

In the preceding program, I incremented the variable x by 1 with the increment operator (++). Using this knowledge, how many times do you think the `printf()` function will execute? To find out, look at Figure 4.9, which depicts the program's output.

FIGURE 4.9

Demonstrating the `while` loop and increment operator (++).

The increment operator (++) is very important for this loop. Without it, an endless loop will occur. In other words, the expression x < 10 will never evaluate to `false`, thus creating an infinite loop.

INFINITE LOOPS

Infinite loops are loops that never end. They are created when a loop's expression is never set to exit the loop.

TIP Every programmer experiences an infinite loop at least once in his or her career. To exit an infinite loop, press Ctrl+C, which produces a break in the program. If this does not work, you may need to end the task.

To end a task on a Windows-based system, press Ctrl+Alt+Del, which should produce a task window or at least allow you to select the Task Manager. From the Task Manager, select the program that contains the infinite loop and choose End Task.

Loops cause the program to do something repeatedly. Think of an ATM's menu. It always reappears when you complete a transaction. How do you think this happens? You can probably guess by now that the programmers who built the ATM software used a form of iteration.

The following program code demonstrates the `while` loop's usefulness in building menus.

```c
#include <stdio.h>

main()
{

    int iSelection = 0;

    while ( iSelection != 4 ) {

        printf("1\tDeposit funds\n");
        printf("2\tWithdraw funds\n");
        printf("3\tPrint Balance\n");
        printf("4\tQuit\n");
        printf("Enter your selection (1-4): ");
        scanf("%d", &iSelection);

    }  //end while loop

    printf("\nThank you\n");

}  //end main function
```

The `while` loop in the preceding program uses a condition to loop as long as the user does not select the number 4. As long as the user selects a valid option other than 4, the menu is displayed repeatedly. If, however, the user selects the number 4, the loop exits and the next statement following the loop's closing brace is executed.

Sample output from the preceding program code is shown in Figure 4.10.

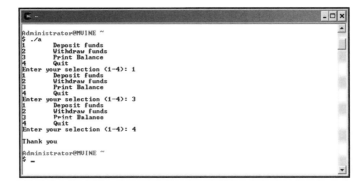

FIGURE 4.10

Building a menu
with the while
loop.

THE DO WHILE LOOP

Similar to the while loop, the do while loop is used to build iteration in your programs. The do while loop, however, has a striking difference from the while loop. The do while loop's condition is at the bottom of the loop rather than at the top. To demonstrate, take another look at the first while loop from the previous section, shown next.

```
while ( x < 10 ) {

    printf("The value of x is %d\n", x);
    x++;

} //end while loop
```

The condition is at the beginning of the while loop. The condition of the do while loop, however, is at the end of the loop, as demonstrated next.

```
do {

    printf("The value of x is %d\n", x);
    x++;

} while ( x < 10 ); //end do while loop
```

CAUTION   In the do while loop's last statement, the ending brace comes before the while statement, and the while statement must end with a semicolon.

If you leave out the semicolon or ending brace or simply rearrange the order of syntax, you are guaranteed a compile error.

Studying the preceding do while loop, can you guess how many times the loop will execute and what the output will look like? If you guessed 10 times, you are correct.

Why use the do while loop instead of the while loop? This is a good question, but it can be answered only by the type of problem being solved. I can, however, show you the importance of choosing each of these loops by studying the next program.

```c
#include <stdio.h>

main()
{

    int x = 10;

    do {

        printf("This printf statement is executed at least once\n");
        x++;

    }  while ( x < 10 ); //end do while loop

    while ( x < 10 ) {

        printf("This printf statement is never executed\n");
        x++;

    }  //end while loop

}  //end main function
```

Using the do while loop allows me to execute the statements inside of my loop at least once, even though the loop's condition will be false when evaluated. The while loop's contents, however, will never execute because the loop's condition is at the top of the loop and will evaluate to false.

THE FOR LOOP

The for loop is an important iteration technique in any programming language. Much different in syntax from its cousins, the while and do while loops, it is much more common for building loops when the number of iterations is already known. The next program block demonstrates a simple for loop.

```c
#include <stdio.h>

main()

{

    int x;

    for ( x = 10; x > 5; x-- )
      printf("The value of x is %d\n", x);

}  //end main function
```

The for loop statement is busier than the other loops I've shown you. A single for loop statement contains three separate expressions, as described in the following bulleted list.

- Variable initialization
- Conditional expression
- Increment/decrement

Using the preceding code, the first expression, variable initialization, initializes the variable to 1. I did not initialize it in the variable declaration statement because it would have been a duplicated and wasted effort. The next expression is a condition (x > 5) that is used to determine when the for loop should stop iterating. The last expression in the for loop (x--) decrements the variable x by 1.

Using this knowledge, how many times do you think the for loop will execute? If you guessed five times, you are correct.

Figure 4.11 depicts the preceding for loop's execution.

FIGURE 4.11

Illustrating the
for loop.

The for loop can also be used when you don't know how many times the loop should execute. To build a for loop without knowing the number of iterations beforehand, you can use a variable as your counter that is assigned by a user. For example, you can build a quiz program that lets the user determine how many questions they would like to answer, which the following program implements.

```c
#include <stdio.h>

main()

{

    int x, iNumQuestions, iResponse, iRndNum1, iRndNum2;
    srand(time());

    printf("\nEnter number of questions to ask: ");
    scanf("%d", &iNumQuestions);

    for ( x = 0; x < iNumQuestions; x++ ) {

        iRndNum1 = rand() % 10 + 1;
        iRndNum2 = rand() % 10 + 1;

        printf("\nWhat is %d x %d: ", iRndNum1, iRndNum2);
        scanf("%d", &iResponse);

        if ( iResponse == iRndNum1 * iRndNum2 )
            printf("\nCorrect!\n");
        else
            printf("\nThe correct answer was %d \n", iRndNum1 * iRndNum2);

    }  //end for loop

}  //end main function
```

In this program code, I first ask the user how many questions he or she would like to answer. But what I'm really asking is how many times my for loop will execute. I use the number of questions derived from the player in my for loop's condition. Using the variable derived from the user, I can dynamically tell my program how many times to loop.

Sample output for this program is shown in Figure 4.12

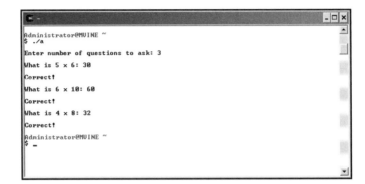

FIGURE 4.12

Determining the
number of
iterations with
user input.

BREAK AND CONTINUE STATEMENTS

The break and continue statements are used to manipulate program flow in structures such
as loops. You may also recall from Chapter 3 that the break statement is used in conjunction
with the switch statement.

When a break statement is executed in a loop, the loop is terminated and program control
returns to the next statement following the end of the loop. The next program statements
demonstrate the use of the break statement.

```c
#include <stdio.h>

main()
{
  int x;

  for ( x = 10; x > 5; x-- ) {

    if ( x == 7 )
       break;

  } //end for loop

  printf("\n%d\n", x);
}
```

In this program, the condition (x == 7) becomes true after the third iteration. Next, the break statement is executed and program control is sent out from the for loop and continues with the printf statement.

The continue statement is also used to manipulate program flow in a loop structure. When executed, though, any remaining statements in the loop are passed over and the next iteration of the loop is sought.

The next program block demonstrates the continue statement.

```c
#include <stdio.h>

main()
{
 int x;

 for ( x = 10; x > 5; x-- ) {

    if ( x == 7 )
      continue;

    printf("\n%d\n", x);

 }  //end for loop
}
```

Notice how the number 7 is not present in the output shown in Figure 4.13. This occurs because when the condition x == 7 is true, the continue statement is executed, thus skipping the printf() function and continuing program flow with the next iteration of the for loop.

FIGURE 4.13

Using the continue statement to alter program flow.

SYSTEM CALLS

Many programming languages provide at least one utility function for accessing operating system commands. C provides one such function, called system. The system function can be used to call all types of UNIX or DOS commands from within C program code. For instance, you could call and execute any of the UNIX commands shown in the following bulleted list.

- ls
- man
- ps
- pwd

For an explanation of these UNIX commands, consult Appendix A, "Common UNIX Commands."

But why call and execute a system command from within a C program? Well, for example, a common dilemma for programmers of text-based languages, such as C, is how to clear the computer's screen. One solution is shown next.

```c
#include <stdio.h>

main()

{

    int x;

    for ( x = 0; x < 25; x++ )
        printf("\n");

}   //end main function
```

This program uses a simple for loop to repeatedly print a new line character. This will eventually clear a computer's screen, but you will have to modify it depending on each computer's setting.

A better solution is to use the system() function to call the UNIX clear command, as demonstrated next.

```c
#include <stdio.h>

main()
```

```
{

   system("clear");

}  //end main function
```

Using the UNIX clear command provides a more fluid experience for your users and is certainly more discernable when evaluating a programmer's intentions.

Try using various UNIX commands with the system function in your own programs. I'm sure you'll find the system function to be useful in at least one of your programs.

CHAPTER PROGRAM: CONCENTRATION

FIGURE 4.14

Using chapter-based concepts to build the Concentration Game.

The Concentration Game uses many of the techniques you learned about in this chapter. Essentially, the Concentration Game generates random numbers and displays them for a short period of time for the user to memorize. During the time the random numbers are displayed, the player tries to memorize the numbers and their sequence. After a few seconds have passed, the computer's screen is cleared and the user is asked to input the same numbers in the same sequence.

The complete code for the Concentration Game is shown next.

```
#include <stdio.h>
#include <stdlib.h>

main()
{

   char cYesNo = '\0';
   int iResp1 = 0;
   int iResp2 = 0;
```

```c
int iResp3 = 0;
int iElaspedTime = 0;
int iCurrentTime = 0;
int iRandomNum = 0;
int i1 = 0;
int i2 = 0;
int i3 = 0;
int iCounter = 0;

srand(time(NULL));

printf("\nPlay a game of Concentration? (y or n): ");
scanf("%c", &cYesNo);

if (cYesNo == 'y' || cYesNo == 'Y') {

    i1 = rand() % 100;
    i2 = rand() % 100;
    i3 = rand() % 100;

    printf("\nConcentrate on the next three numbers\n");
    printf("\n%d\t%d\t%d\n", i1, i2, i3);

    iCurrentTime = time(NULL);

    do {

       iElaspedTime = time(NULL);

    } while ( (iElaspedTime - iCurrentTime) < 3 ); //end do while loop

    system ("clear");

    printf("\nEnter each # separated with one space: ");
    scanf("%d%d%d", &iResp1, &iResp2, &iResp3);

    if ( i1 == iResp1 && i2 == iResp2 && i3 == iResp3 )
       printf("\nCongratulations!\n");
```

```
    else
       printf("\nSorry, correct numbers were %d %d %d\n", i1, i2, i3);

    }  //end if
}  //end main function
```

Try this game out for yourself; I'm certain you and your friends will like it. For more ideas on how to enhance the Concentration Game, see the "Challenges" section at the end of this chapter.

SUMMARY

- Looping structures use conditional expressions (conditions) to evaluate how many times something happens.
- You can differentiate between conditions and loops in flowcharts by looking at the program flow. Specifically, if you see connector lines that loop back to the beginning of a condition (diamond symbol), you know that the condition represents a loop.
- The ++ operator is useful for incrementing number-based variables by 1.
- The -- operator decrements number-based variables by 1.
- Both the increment and decrement operators can be placed on both sides (prefix and postfix) of variable, which produces different results.
- The += operator adds a variable's contents to another variable.
- The -= operator subtracts the contents of a variable from another variable.
- A loop's beginning and ending braces are required only when more than one statement is included in the loop's body.
- Infinite loops are created when a loop's expression is never set to exit the loop.
- The do while loop's condition is at the bottom of the loop rather than at the top.
- The for loop is common for building loops when the number of iterations is already known or can be known prior to execution.
- When executed, the break statement terminates a loop's execution and returns program control back to the next statement following the end of the loop.
- When executed, the continue statement passes over any remaining statements in the loop and continues to the next iteration in the loop.
- The system() function can be used to call operating system commands such as the UNIX clear command.

CHALLENGES

1. Create a counting program that counts from 1 to 100 in increments of 5.

2. Create a counting program that counts backward from 100 to 1 in increments of 10.

3. Create a counting program that prompts the user for three inputs (shown next) that determine how and what to count. Store the user's answers in variables. Use the acquired data to build your counting program with a for loop and display the results to the user.

   - Beginning number to start counting from

   - Ending number to stop counting at

   - Increment number

4. Create a math quiz program that prompts the user for how many questions to ask. The program should congratulate the player if he or she gets the correct answer or alert the user of the correct answer in the event the question is answered incorrectly.
   The math quiz program should also keep track of how many questions the player has answered correctly and incorrectly and display these running totals at the end of the quiz.

5. Modify the Concentration Game to use a main menu. The menu should allow the user to select a level of difficulty and/or quit the game (a sample menu is shown below). The level of difficulty could be determined by how many separate numbers the user has to concentrate on and/or how many seconds the player has to concentrate. Each time the user completes a single game of Concentration, the menu should reappear allowing the user to continue at the same level, at a new level, or simply quit the game.

   1   Easy (remember 3 numbers in 5 seconds)
   2   Intermediate (remember 5 numbers in 5 seconds)
   3   Difficult (remember 5 numbers in 2 seconds)
   4   Quit

STRUCTURED PROGRAMMING

A concept steeped in computer programming history, *structured programming* enables programmers to break problems into small and easily understood components that eventually will comprise a complete system. In this chapter, I will show you how to use structured programming concepts, such as top-down design, and programming techniques, such as creating your own functions, to build efficient and reusable code in your programs.

This chapter specifically covers the following topics:

- Introduction to structured programming
- Function prototypes
- Function definitions
- Function calls
- Variable scope

INTRODUCTION TO STRUCTURED PROGRAMMING

Structured programming enables programmers to break complex systems into manageable components. In C, these components are known as *functions*, which are at the heart of this chapter. In this section I will give you background on common structured programming techniques and concepts. After reading this section, you will be ready to build your own C functions.

Structured programming contains many concepts ranging from theoretical to application. Many of these concepts are intuitive, whereas others will take a while to sink in and take root.

The most relevant structured programming concepts for this text are the following:

- Top-down design
- Code reusability
- Information hiding

Top-Down Design

Common with procedural languages such as C, *top-down design* enables analysts and program-mers to define detailed statements about a system's specific tasks. Top-down design experts argue that humans are limited in their multitasking capabilities. Those who excel at multi-tasking and enjoy the chaos it brings are generally not programmers. Programmers are inclined to work on a single problem with tedious detail.

To demonstrate top-down design, I'll use an ATM (Automated Teller Machine) as an example. Suppose your non-technical boss tells you to program the software for a new ATM system for the Big Money Bank. You would probably wonder where to begin as it's a large task filled with complexities and many details.

Top-down design can help you design your way out of the dark and treacherous forest of systems design. The following steps demonstrate the top-down design process.

1. Break the problem into small, manageable components, starting from the top. In C, the top component is the `main()` function from which other components are called.
2. Identify all major components. For the ATM example, assume there are four major components:

   - Display balance
   - Deposit funds
   - Transfer funds
   - Withdraw funds

3. Now that you have separated the major system components, you can visualize the work involved. Decompose one major component at a time and make it more manageable and less complex.

4. The withdraw funds component can be broken down into smaller pieces, such as these:

- Get available balance
- Compare available balance to amount requested
- Update customer's account
- Distribute approved funds
- Reject request
- Print receipt

5. Go even further with the decomposition process and divide the "distribute approved funds" component even smaller:

- Verify ATM funds exist
- Initiate mechanical processes
- Update bank records

Figure 5.1 depicts a sample process for decomposing the ATM system.

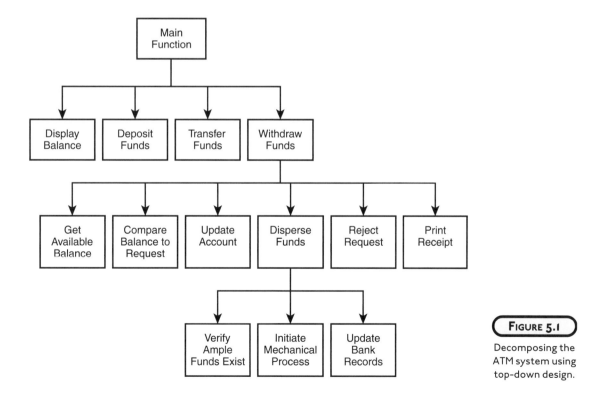

FIGURE 5.1

Decomposing the ATM system using top-down design.

With my ATM system decomposed into manageable components, I feel a bit less feverish about the forthcoming programming tasks. Moreover, I can now assign myself smaller, more manageable components to start programming.

I hope you see how much easier it is to think about implementing a single component, such as verifying ATM funds exist, than the daunting task of building an entire ATM system. Moreover, at the decomposed level, multiple programmers can work on the same system without knowing the immediate details of each other's programming tasks.

During your programming career, I'm certain you will be faced with similar complex ideas that need to be implemented with programming languages. If used properly, top-down design can be a useful tool for making your problems easier to understand and implement.

Code Reusability

In the world of application development, code reusability is implemented as functions in C. Specifically, programmers create user-defined functions for problems that generally need frequently used solutions. To demonstrate, consider the following list of components and subcomponents from the ATM example in the previous section.

- Get available balance
- Compare available balance to amount requested
- Update customer's account
- Distribute approved funds
- Reject request
- Print receipt

Given the ATM system, how many times do you think the update customer account problem would occur for any one customer or transaction? Depending on the ATM system, the update customer account component can be called a number of times. A customer can perform many transactions while at an ATM. The following list demonstrates a possible number of transactions a customer might perform at a single visit to an ATM.

- Deposit monies into a checking account
- Transfer funds from a checking to a savings account
- Withdraw monies from checking
- Print balance

At least four occasions require you to access the customer's balance. Writing code structures every time you need to access someone's balance doesn't make sense, because you can write a function that contains the logic and structures to handle this procedure and then reuse that function when needed. Putting all the code into one function that can be called repeatedly will save you programming time immediately and in the future if changes to the function need to be made.

Let me discuss another example using the printf() function (which you are already familiar with) that demonstrates code reuse. In this example, a programmer has already implemented the code and structures needed to print plain text to standard output. You simply use the printf() function by calling its name and passing the desired characters to it. Because the printf() function exists in a module or library, you can call it repeatedly without knowing its implementation details, or, in other words, how it was built. Code reuse is truly a programmer's best friend!

Information Hiding

Information hiding is a conceptual process by which programmers conceal implementation details into functions. Functions can be seen as black boxes. A black box is simply a component, logical or physical, that performs a task. You don't know how the black box performs (implements) the task; you just simply know it works when needed. Figure 5.2 depicts the black box concept.

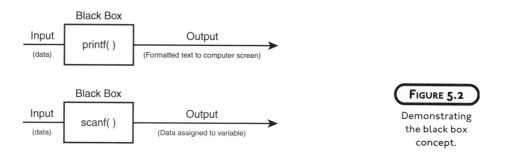

FIGURE 5.2

Demonstrating the black box concept.

Consider the two black box drawings in Figure 5.2. Each black box describes one component; in this case the components are printf() and scanf(). The reason that I consider the two functions printf() and scanf() black boxes is because you do not need to know what's inside of them (how they are made), you only need to know what they take as input and what they return as output. In other words, understanding how to use a function while not knowing how it is built is a good example of information hiding.

Many of the functions you have used so far demonstrate the usefulness of information hiding. Table 5.1 lists more common library functions that implement information hiding in structured programming.

	TABLE 5.1	COMMON LIBRARY FUNCTIONS	

Library Name	Function Name	Description
Standard input/output	scanf()	Reads data from the keyboard
Standard input/output	printf()	Prints data to the computer monitor
Character handling	isdigit()	Tests for decimal digit characters
Character handling	islower()	Tests for lowercase letters
Character handling	isupper()	Tests for uppercase letters
Character handling	tolower()	Converts character to lowercase
Character handling	toupper()	Converts character to uppercase
Mathematics	exp()	Computes the exponential
Mathematics	pow()	Computes a number raised to a power
Mathematics	sqrt()	Computes the square root

If you're still put off by the notion of information hiding or black boxes, consider the following question. Do most people know how a car's engine works? Probably not, most people are only concerned that they know how to operate a car. Fortunately, modern cars provide an interface from which you can easily use the car, while hiding its implementation details. In other words, one might consider the car's engine the black box. You only know what the black box takes as input (gas) and what it gives as output (motion).

Going back to the printf() function, what do you really know about it? You know that the printf() function prints characters you supply to the computer's screen. But do you know how the printf() function really works? Probably not, and you don't need to. That's a key concept of information hiding.

In structured programming you build components that can be reused (code reusability) and that include an interface that other programmers will know how to use without needing to understand how they were built (information hiding).

FUNCTION PROTOTYPES

Function prototypes tell C how your function will be built and used. It is a common programming practice to construct your function prototype before the actual function is built. That statement was so important it is worth noting again. **It is common programming practice to construct your function prototype before the actual function is built.**

Programmers must think about the desired purpose of the function, how it will receive input, and how and what it will return. To demonstrate, take a look at the following function prototype.

```
float addTwoNumbers(int, int);
```

This function prototype tells C the following things about the function:

- The data type returned by the function—in this case a `float` data type is returned
- The number of parameters received—in this case two
- The data types of the parameters—in this case both parameters are integer data types
- The order of the parameters

Function implementations and their prototypes can vary. It is not always necessary to send input as parameters to functions, nor is it always necessary to have functions return values. In these cases, programmers say the functions are void of parameters and/or are void of a return value. The next two function prototypes demonstrate the concept of functions with the `void` keyword.

```
void printBalance(int);   //function prototype
```

The `void` keyword in the preceding example tells C that the function `printBalance` will not return a value. In other words, this function is void of a return value.

```
int createRandomNumber(void);   //function prototype
```

The `void` keyword in the parameter list of the `createRandomNumber` function tells C this function will not accept any parameters, but it will return an integer value. In other words, this function is void of parameters.

Function prototypes should be placed outside the `main()` function and before the `main()` function starts, as demonstrated next.

```
#include <stdio.h>

int addTwoNumbers(int, int);   //function prototype

main()
{

}
```

There is no limit to the number of function prototypes you can include in your C program. Consider the next block of code, which implements four function prototypes.

```
#include <stdio.h>

int addTwoNumbers(int, int);   //function prototype
int subtractTwoNumbers(int, int);   //function prototype
int divideTwoNumbers(int, int);   //function prototype
int multiplyTwoNumbers(int, int);   //function prototype

main()

{

}
```

FUNCTION DEFINITIONS

I have shown you how C programmers create the blueprints for user-defined functions with function prototypes. In this section, I will show you how to build user-defined functions using the function prototypes.

Function definitions implement the function prototype. In fact, the first line of the function definition (also known as the header) resembles the function prototype, with minor exceptions. To demonstrate, study the next block of code.

```
#include <stdio.h>

int addTwoNumbers(int, int);   //function prototype

main()

{

    printf("Nothing happening in here.");

}

//function definition
int addTwoNumbers(int operand1, int operand2)
{
```

```
    return operand1 + operand2;


}
```

I have two separate and complete functions: the `main()` function and the `addTwoNumbers()` function. The function prototype and the first line of the function definition (the function header) bear a striking resemblance. The only difference is that the function header contains actual variable names for parameters and the function prototype contains only the variable data type. The function definition does not contain a semicolon after the header (unlike its prototype). Similar to the `main()` function, the function definition must include a beginning and ending brace.

In C, functions can return a value to the calling statement. To return a value, use the `return` keyword, which initiates the return value process. In the next section, you will learn how to call a function that receives its return value.

 You can use the keyword `return` in one of two fashions: First, you can use the `return` keyword to pass a value or expression result back to the calling statement. Second, you can use the keyword `return` without any values or expressions to return program control back to the calling statement.

Sometimes however, it is not necessary for a function to return any value. For example, the next program builds a function simply to compare the values of two numbers.

```
//function definition
int compareTwoNumbers(int num1, int num2)
{

  if (num1 < num2)
     printf("\n%d is less than %d\n", num1, num2);
  else if (num1 == num2)
    printf("\n%d is equal to %d\n", num1, num2);
  else
    printf("\n%d is greater than %d\n", num1, num2);


}
```

Notice in the preceding function definition that the function `compareTwoNumbers()` does not return a value. To further demonstrate the process of building functions, study the next program that builds a report header.

```
//function definition
void printReportHeader()
{

    printf("\nColumn1\tColumn2\tColumn3\tColumn4\n");

}
```

To build a program that implements multiple function definitions, build each function definition as stated in each function prototype. The next program implements the main() function, which does nothing of importance, and then builds two functions to perform basic math operations and return a result.

```
#include <stdio.h>

int addTwoNumbers(int, int);  //function prototype
int subtractTwoNumbers(int, int);  //function prototype

main()

{

    printf("Nothing happening in here.");

}

//function definition
int addTwoNumbers(int num1, int num2)
{

    return num1 + num2;

}

//function definition
int subtractTwoNumbers(int num1, int num2)
{
```

```
    return num1 - num2;


}
```

FUNCTION CALLS

It's now time to put your functions to work with function calls. Up to this point, you may have been wondering how you or your program will use these functions. You work with your user-defined functions the same way you work with other C library functions such as printf() and scanf().

Using the addTwoNumbers() function from the previous section, I include a single function call in my main() function as shown next.

```
#include <stdio.h>

int addTwoNumbers(int, int);  //function prototype

main()

{

    int iResult;

    iResult = addTwoNumbers(5, 5); //function call

}

//function definition
int addTwoNumbers(int operand1, int operand2)
{

    return operand1 + operand2;

}
```

addTwoNumbers(5, 5) calls the function and passes it two integer parameters. When C encounters a function call, it redirects program control to the function definition. If the function definition returns a value, the entire function call statement is replaced by the return value.

In other words, the entire statement addTwoNumbers(5, 5) is replaced with the number 10. In the preceding program, the returned value of 10 is assigned to the integer variable iResult.

Function calls can also be placed in other functions. To demonstrate, study the next block of code that uses the same addTwoNumbers() function call inside a printf() function.

```c
#include <stdio.h>

int addTwoNumbers(int, int);   //function prototype

main()

{

   printf("\nThe result is %d", addTwoNumbers(5, 5));

}

//function definition
int addTwoNumbers(int operand1, int operand2)
{

   return operand1 + operand2;

}
```

In the preceding function call, I hard-coded two numbers as parameters. You can be more dynamic with function calls by passing variables as parameters, as shown next.

```c
#include <stdio.h>

int addTwoNumbers(int, int);   //function prototype

main()

{

   int num1, num2;

   printf("\nEnter the first number: ");
```

```
    scanf("%d", &num1);
    printf("\nEnter the second number: ");
    scanf("%d", &num2);

    printf("\nThe result is %d\n", addTwoNumbers(num1, num2));

}
//function definition
int addTwoNumbers(int operand1, int operand2)
{

    return operand1 + operand2;

}
```

The output of the preceding program is shown in Figure 5.3.

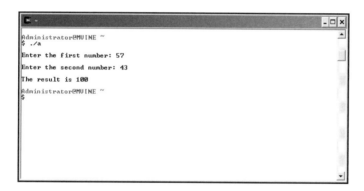

FIGURE 5.3

Passing variables as parameters to user-defined functions.

Demonstrated next is the `printReportHeader()` function that prints a report header using the \t escape sequence to print a tab between words.

```
#include <stdio.h>

void printReportHeader();   //function prototype

main()

{
```

```
    printReportHeader();

}

//function definition
void printReportHeader()
{

    printf("\nColumn1\tColumn2\tColumn3\tColumn4\n");

}
```

Calling a function that requires no parameters or returns no value is as simple as calling its name with empty parentheses.

Failing to use parentheses in function calls void of parameters can result in compile errors or invalid program operations. Consider the two following function calls.

```
printReportHeader;     //Incorrect function call
printReportHeader();    //Correct function call
```

The first function call will not cause a compile error but will fail to execute the function call to printReportHeader. The second function call, however, contains the empty parentheses and will successfully call printReportHeader().

VARIABLE SCOPE

Variable scope identifies and determines the life span of any variable in any programming language. When a variable loses its scope, it means its data value is lost. I will discuss two common types of variables scopes in C, local and global, so you will better understand the importance of variable scope.

Local Scope

You have unknowingly been using local scope variables since Chapter 2, "Primary Data Types." Local variables are defined in functions, such as the main() function, and lose their scope each time the function is executed, as shown in the following program:

```
#include <stdio.h>

main()
```

```
{

    int num1;

    printf("\nEnter a number: ");
    scanf("%d", &num1);
    printf("\nYou entered %d\n ", num1);

}
```

Each time the preceding program is run, C allocates memory space for the integer variable num1 with its variable declaration. Data stored in the variable is lost when the main() function is terminated.

Because local scope variables are tied to their originating functions, you can reuse variable names in other functions without running the risk of overwriting data. To demonstrate, review the following program code and its output in Figure 5.4.

```
#include <stdio.h>

int getSecondNumber();   //function prototype

main()

{

    int num1;

    printf("\nEnter a number: ");
    scanf("%d", &num1);
    printf("\nYou entered %d and %d\n ", num1, getSecondNumber());

}

//function definition
int getSecondNumber ()
{

    int num1;
```

```
    printf("\nEnter a second number: ");
    scanf("%d", &num1);

    return num1;

}
```

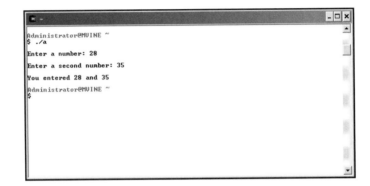

FIGURE 5.4

Using the same
local scope
variable name in
different
functions.

Because the variable num1 is scoped locally to each function, there are no concerns or issues with overwriting data. Specifically, the num1 variable in each function is a separate memory address, and therefore each is a unique variable.

Global Scope

Locally scoped variables can be reused in other functions without harming one another's contents. At times, however, you might want to share data between and across functions. To support the concept of sharing data, you can create and use *global variables*.

Global variables are created and defined outside any function, including the main() function. To show how global variables work, examine the next program.

```
#include <stdio.h>

void printLuckyNumber();  //function prototype

int iLuckyNumber;   //global variable

main()

{
```

```
    printf("\nEnter your lucky number: ");
    scanf("%d", &iLuckyNumber);
    printLuckyNumber();

}
//function definition
void printLuckyNumber()
{

    printf("\nYour lucky number is: %d\n", iLuckyNumber);

}
```

The variable iLuckyNumber is global because it is created outside any function, including the main() function. I can assign data to the global variable in one function and reference the same memory space in another function. It is not wise, however, to use global variables liberally as they can be error prone and deviate from protecting data. Using global variables allows all functions in a program file to have access to the same data, which goes against the concept of information hiding.

CHAPTER PROGRAM—TRIVIA

As demonstrated in Figure 5.5, the Trivia game utilizes many of this chapter's concepts and techniques.

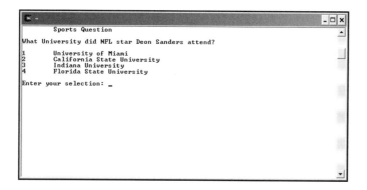

FIGURE 5.5

Demonstrating chapter-based concepts with the Trivia game.

The Trivia game uses function prototypes, function definitions, function calls, and a global variable to build a simple and fun game. Players select a trivia category from the main menu and are asked a question. The program replies that the answer is correct or incorrect.

Each trivia category is broken down into a function that implements the question and answer logic. There is also a user-defined function, which builds a pause utility.

All of the code necessary for building the Trivia game is shown next.

```c
#include <stdio.h>

/********************************************
FUNCTION PROTOTYPES
********************************************/
int sportsQuestion(void);
int geographyQuestion(void);
void pause(int);
/********************************************/


/********************************************
GLOBAL VARIABLE
********************************************/
int giResponse = 0;
/********************************************/
main()

{

    do {

        system("clear");
        printf("\n\tTHE TRIVIA GAME\n\n");
        printf("1\tSports\n");
        printf("2\tGeography\n");
        printf("3\tQuit\n");
        printf("\n\nEnter your selection: ");
        scanf("%d", &giResponse);

        switch(giResponse) {

            case 1:

                if (sportsQuestion() == 4)
```

```
                        printf("\nCorrect!\n");
                else
                    printf("\nIncorrect\n");

                pause(2);
                break;

            case 2:

                if (geographyQuestion() == 2)
                    printf("\nCorrect!\n");
                else
                    printf("\nIncorrect\n");

                pause(2);
                break;

        }   //end switch

    }   while ( giResponse != 3 );

} //end main function


/***********************************************************
FUNCTION DEFINITION
***********************************************************/
int sportsQuestion(void)
{

    int iAnswer = 0;

    system("clear");
    printf("\tSports Question\n");
    printf("\nWhat University did NFL star Deon Sanders attend? ");
    printf("\n\n1\tUniversity of Miami\n");
    printf("2\tCalifornia State University\n");
    printf("3\tIndiana University\n");
    printf("4\tFlorida State University\n");
```

```
    printf("\nEnter your selection: ");
    scanf("%d", &iAnswer);

    return iAnswer;

} //end sportsQuestion function


/************************************************************
FUNCTION DEFINITION
************************************************************/
int geographyQuestion(void)
{

    int iAnswer = 0;

    system("clear");
    printf("\tGeography Question\n");
    printf("\nWhat is the state capitol of Florida? ");
    printf("\n\n1\tPensecola\n");
    printf("2\tTallahassee\n");
    printf("3\tJacksonville\n");
    printf("4\tMiami\n");
    printf("\nEnter your selection: ");
    scanf("%d", &iAnswer);

    return iAnswer;

} //end geographyQuestion function


/************************************************************
FUNCTION DEFINITION
************************************************************/
void pause(int inNum)
{

    int iCurrentTime = 0;
    int iElapsedTime = 0;
```

```
iCurrentTime = time(NULL);

  do {

    iElapsedTime = time(NULL);

  } while ( (iElapsedTime - iCurrentTime) < inNum );

} // end pause function
```

SUMMARY

- Structured programming enables programmers to break complex systems into manageable components.
- Top-down design breaks the problem into small, manageable components, starting from the top.
- Code reusability is implemented as functions in C.
- Information hiding is a conceptual process by which programmers conceal implementation details into functions.
- Function prototypes tell C how your function will be built and used.
- It is common programming practice to construct your function prototype before the actual function is built.
- Function prototypes tell C the data type returned by the function, the number of parameters received, the data types of the parameters, and the order of the parameters.
- Function definitions implement the function prototype.
- In C, functions can return a value to the calling statement. To return a value, use the `return` keyword, which initiates the return value process.
- You can use the `return` keyword to pass a value or expression result back to the calling statement or you can use the keyword `return` without any values or expressions to return program control back to the calling statement.
- Failing to use parentheses in function calls void of parameters can result in compile errors or invalid program operations.
- Variable scope identifies and determines the life span of any variable in any programming language. When a variable loses its scope, its data value is lost.
- Local variables are defined in functions, such as the `main()` function, and lose their scope each time the function is executed.

- Locally scoped variables can be reused in other functions without harming one another's contents.
- Global variables are created and defined outside any function, including the main() function.

CHALLENGES

1. Write a function prototype for the following components:

   - A function that divides two numbers and returns the remainder

   - A function that finds the larger of two numbers and returns the result

   - A function that prints an ATM menu—it receives no parameters and returns no value

2. Build the function definitions for each preceding function prototype.

3. Add your own trivia categories to the Trivia game.

4. Modify the Trivia game to track the number of times a user gets an answer correct and incorrect. When the user quits the program, display the number of correct and incorrect answers. Consider using global variables to track the number of questions answered, the number answered correctly, and the number answered incorrectly.

ARRAYS

An important and versatile programming construct, *arrays* allow you to build collections of like variables. This chapter will cover many array topics, such as creating single and multidimensional arrays, initializing them, and searching through their contents. Specifically, this chapter covers the following array topics:

- Introduction to arrays
- One-dimensional arrays
- Two-dimensional arrays

INTRODUCTION TO ARRAYS

Just as with loops and conditions, arrays are a common programming construct and an important concept for beginning programmers to learn. Arrays can be found in most high-level programming languages, such as C, and offer a simple way of grouping like variables for easy access. Arrays in C share a few common attributes as shown next.

- Variables in an array share the same name
- Variables in an array share the same data type

- Individual variables in an array are called *elements*
- Elements in an array are accessed with an index number

Like any other variable, arrays occupy memory space. Moreover, an array is a grouping of contiguous memory segments, as demonstrated in Figure 6.1.

FIGURE 6.1

A six-element array.

The six-element array in Figure 6.1 starts with index 0. This is an important concept to remember, so it's worth repeating. *Elements in an array begin with index number zero.* There are six array elements in Figure 6.1, starting with element 0 and ending with element 5.

A common programming error is to not account for the zero-based index in arrays. This programming error is often called the off-by-one error. This type of error is generally not caught during compile time, but rather at run time when a user or your program attempts to access an element number of an array that does not exist. For example, if you have a six-element array and your program tries to access the sixth element with index number six, either a run-time program error will ensue or data may be lost. This is because the last index in a six-element array is index 5.

ONE-DIMENSIONAL ARRAYS

There are occasions when you might need or want to use a one-dimensional array. Although there is no rule for when to use an array, some problems are better suited for an array-based solution, as demonstrated in the following list.

- The number of pages in each chapter of a book
- A list of students' GPAs
- Keeping track of your golf score
- A list of phone numbers

Looking at the preceding list, you may be wondering why you would use an array to store the aforementioned information. Consider the golf score statement. If you created a program that kept track of your golf scores, how many variables, or better yet variable names, would you need to store a score for each hole in a golf game? If you solved this question with individual variables, your variable declarations may resemble the following code:

```
int iHole1, iHole2, iHole3, iHole4, iHole5, iHole6;
int iHole7, iHole8, iHole9, iHole10, iHole11, iHole12;
int iHole13, iHole14, iHole15, iHole16, iHole17, iHole18;
```

Whew! That's a lot of variables to keep track of. If you use an array, you only need one variable name with 18 elements, as shown next.

```
int iGolfScores[18];
```

Creating One-Dimensional Arrays

Creating and using one-dimensional arrays is easy, though it may take some time and practice for it to become that way. Arrays in C are created in similar fashion to other variables, as shown next.

```
int iArray[10];
```

The preceding declaration creates a single-dimension, integer-based array called `iArray`, which contains 10 elements. Remember that arrays are zero-based; you start counting with the number zero up to the number defined in the brackets minus 1 (0, 1, 2, 3, 4, 5, 6, 7, 8, 9 gives you 10 elements).

Arrays can be declared to contain other data types as well. To demonstrate, consider the next array declarations using various data types.

```
float fAverages[30];   //Float data type array with 30 elements
double dResults[3];    //Double data type array with 3 elements
short sSalaries[9];    //Short data type array with 9 elements
char cName[19];  //Char array - 18 character elements and one null character
```

Initializing One-Dimensional Arrays

In C, memory spaces are not cleared from their previous value when variables or arrays are created. Because of this, it is generally good programming practice to not only initialize your variables but to also initialize your arrays.

There are two ways to initialize your arrays: within the array declaration and outside of the array declaration. In the first way, you simply assign one or more comma-separated values within braces to the array in the array's declaration.

```
int iArray[5] = {0, 1, 2, 3, 4};
```

Placing numbers inside braces and separating them by commas will assign a default value to each respective element number.

> **TIP**
>
> You can quickly initialize your arrays with a single default value as demonstrated in the following array declaration.
>
> ```
> int iArray[5] = {0};
> ```
>
> Assigning the single numeric value of 0 in an array declaration will, by default, assign all array elements the value of 0.

Another way to initialize your array elements is to use looping structures such as the `for` loop. To demonstrate, examine the following program code.

```
#include <stdio.h>

main()

{

    int x;
    int iArray[5];

    for ( x = 0; x < 5; x++ )
        iArray[x] = 0;

}
```

In the preceding program, I've declared two variables, one integer variable called `x`, which is used in the `for` loop, and one integer-based array called `iArray`. Because I know I have five elements in my array, I need to iterate five times in my `for` loop. Within my loop, I assign the number zero to each element of the array, which are easily accessed with the counter variable `x` inside of my assignment statement.

To print the entire contents of an array, you also will need to use a looping structure, as demonstrated in the next program.

```
#include <stdio.h>

main()

{
```

```
   int x;
   int iArray[5];

//initialize array elements
   for ( x = 0; x < 5; x++ )
      iArray[x] = x;

//print array element contents
   for ( x = 0; x < 5; x++ )
      printf("\nThe value of iArray index %d is %d\n", x, x);


}
```

I initialize the preceding array called iArray differently by assigning the value of the x variable to each array element. I will get a different value for each array element, as shown in Figure 6.2, because the x variable is incremented each time the loop iterates. After initializing the array, I use another for loop to print the contents of the array.

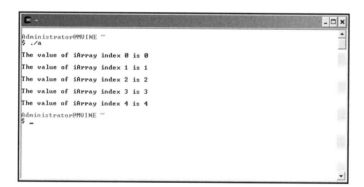

FIGURE 6.2

Printing the contents of an array.

There are times when you only need to access a single element of an array. This can be accomplished in one of two manners: hard-coding a number value for the index or using variables. Hard-coding a number value for the index is shown in the next printf() function.

```
printf("\nThe value of index 4 is %d\n", iArray[3]);
```

Hard-coding the index value of an array assumes that you will always need or want the element number. A more dynamic way of accessing a single element number is to use variables. In the next program block, I use the input of a user to access a single array element's value.

```
#include <stdio.h>

main()

{

    int x;
    int iIndex = -1;
    int iArray[5];

    for ( x = 0; x < 5; x++ )
        iArray[x] = (x + 5);

    do {

        printf("\nEnter a valid index (0-4): ");
        scanf("%d", &iIndex);

    } while ( iIndex < 0 || iIndex > 4 );

    printf("\nThe value of index %d is %d\n", iIndex, iArray[iIndex]);

}   //end main
```

I mix up the array initialization in the `for` loop by adding the integer five to the value of x
each time the loop iterates. However, I must perform more work when getting an index value
from the user. Basically, I test that the user has entered a valid index number; otherwise my
program will give invalid results. To validate the user's input, I insert `printf()` and `scanf()`
functions inside a `do while` loop and iterate until I get a valid value, after which I can print
the desired element contents. Figure 6.3 demonstrates the output of the preceding program
block.

Character arrays should also be initialized before using them. Elements in a character array
hold characters plus a special null termination character, which is represented by the character constant '/0'. Character arrays can be initialized in a number of ways. For instance, the
following code initializes an array with a predetermined character sequence.

```
char cName[] = { 'O', 'l', 'i', 'v', 'i', 'a', '\0' };
```

```
Administrator@MUINE ~
$ ./a

Enter a valid index (0-4): 4

The value of index 4 is 9

Administrator@MUINE ~
$
```

FIGURE 6.3

Accessing one
element of an
array with a
variable.

The preceding array declaration creates an array called cName with seven elements, including the null character '/0'. Another way of initializing the same cName array is revealed next.

```
char cName[] = "Olivia";
```

Initializing a character array with a character sequence surrounded by double quotes appends the null character automatically.

CAUTION When creating character arrays, be sure to allocate enough room to store the largest character sequence assignable. Also, remember to allow enough room in the character array to store the null character ('\0').

Study the next program, with output shown in Figure 6.4, which demonstrates the creation of two character arrays—one initialized and the other not.

```c
#include <stdio.h>

main()

{

    int x;
    char cArray[5];
    char cName[] = "Olivia";

    printf("\nCharacter array not initialized:\n");

    for ( x = 0; x < 5; x++ )
        printf("Element %d's contents are %d\n", x, cArray[x]);
```

```
        printf("\nInitialized character array:\n");

    for ( x = 0; x < 6; x++ )
        printf("%c", cName[x]);

}  //end main
```

Figure 6.4 demonstrates why it is necessary to initialize arrays because old data may already exist in each element. In the case of Figure 6.4, you can see leftover data (not assigned nor initialized by me) stored in the cArray's elements.

FIGURE 6.4

Initializing a character-based array.

Searching One-Dimensional Arrays

One of the most common practices with arrays is searching their elements for contents. Once again, you will use looping structures, such as the for loop, to iterate through each element until the search value is found or the search is over.

The concept of searching an array is demonstrated in the next program, which prompts a user to enter a numeric search value.

```
#include <stdio.h>

main()

{

    int x;
    int iValue;
    int iFound = -1;
    int iArray[5];
```

```
for ( x = 0; x < 5; x++ )
   iArray[x] = (x + x);    //initialize array

printf("\nEnter value to search for: ");
scanf("%d", &iValue);

for ( x = 0; x < 5; x++ ) {

   if ( iArray[x] == iValue ) {
      iFound = x;
      break;
   }

} //end for loop

if ( iFound > -1 )
   printf("\nI found your search value in element %d\n", iFound);
else
   printf("\nSorry, your search value was not found\n");

} //end main
```

As the preceding program shows, I use two separate loops: one for initializing my integer-based array to the counting variable plus itself (iArray[x] = (x + x)) and the other, which searches the array using the user's search value.

Valid values for each preceding array element are shown in Table 6.1.

TABLE 6.1   VALID ELEMENT VALUES FOR iARRAY[x] = (x + x)

Element Number	Value after Initialization
0	0
1	2
2	4
3	6
4	8

If a match is found, I assign the element to a variable and exit the loop with the break keyword. After the search process, I alert the user if the value was found and at which element number. If no match was found, I also alert the user.

Figure 6.5 demonstrates the output of the searching program.

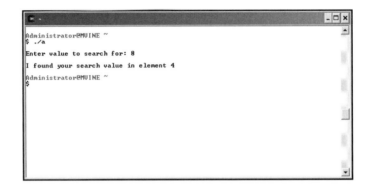

FIGURE 6.5

Searching the
contents of an
array.

Remember that the break keyword can be used to exit a loop early. When C encounters the break keyword in a loop, it moves program control to the next statement outside of the loop. This can be a timesaving advantage when searching through large amounts of information.

TWO-DIMENSIONAL ARRAYS

Two-dimensional arrays are even more interesting structures than their single-dimension counterparts. The easiest way to understand or think about two-dimensional arrays is to visualize a table with rows and columns (e.g. a checkerboard, chessboard, or spreadsheet). C, however, implements two-dimensional arrays as single-dimension arrays with pointers to other single-dimension arrays. For ease of understanding, though, envision two-dimensional arrays as a grid or table as mentioned previously.

Two-dimensional arrays are created similar to one-dimensional arrays, but with one exception: two-dimensional arrays must be declared with two separate element numbers (number of columns and number of rows) as shown next.

```
int iTwoD[3][3];
```

The array declaration above creates a total of 9 elements (remember that array indexes start with number 0). Two-dimensional arrays are accessed with two element numbers, one for the column and one for the row.

Figure 6.6 demonstrates a two-dimensional array with nine elements.

	Column 0	Column 1	Column 2
Row 0	iTwoD[0][0]	iTwoD[0][1]	iTwoD[0][2]
Row 1	iTwoD[1][0]	iTwoD[1][1]	iTwoD[1][2]
Row 2	iTwoD[2][0]	iTwoD[2][1]	iTwoD[2][2]

FIGURE 6.6

Two-dimensional
array described.

Initializing Two-Dimensional Arrays

You can initialize a two-dimensional array in a couple of ways. First, you can initialize a two-dimensional array in its declaration, as shown next.

```
int iTwoD[3][3] = { {0, 1, 2}, {0, 1, 2}, {0, 1, 2} };
```

Each grouping of braces initializes a single row of elements. For example, iTwoD[0][0] gets 0, iTwoD[0][1] gets 1, and iTwoD[0][2] gets 2. Table 6.2 demonstrates the values assigned to the preceding two-dimensional array.

TABLE 6.2   TWO-DIMENSIONAL ARRAY VALUES AFTER INITIALIZING

Element Reference	Value
iTwoD[0][0]	0
iTwoD[0][1]	1
iTwoD[0][2]	2
iTwoD[1][0]	0
iTwoD[1][1]	1
iTwoD[1][2]	2
iTwoD[2][0]	0
iTwoD[2][1]	1
iTwoD[2][2]	2

You can also use looping structures, such as the for loop, to initialize your two-dimensional arrays. As you might expect, there is a bit more work when initializing or searching a two-dimensional array. Essentially, you must create a nested looping structure for searching or accessing each element, as shown in the next program.

```
#include <stdio.h>

main()

{
```

```
int iTwoD[3][3];
int x, y;

//intialize the 2-d array
for ( x = 0; x <= 2; x++ ) {

    for ( y = 0; y <= 2; y++ )
        iTwoD[x][y] = ( x + y );

}  //end outer loop

//print the 2-d array
for ( x = 0; x <= 2; x++ ) {

    for ( y = 0; y <= 2; y++ )
        printf("iTwoD[%d][%d] = %d\n", x, y, iTwoD[x][y]);

} //end outer loop

} //end main
```

Nested loops are necessary to search through a two-dimensional array. In the preceding example, my first combination of looping structures initializes each element to variable x plus variable y. Moreover, the outer loop controls the number of iterations through the rows (three rows in all). Once inside the first loop, my inner loop takes over and iterates three times for each outer loop. The inner loop uses a separate variable, y, to loop through each column number of the current row (three columns in each row). The last grouping of loops accesses each element and prints to standard output using the printf() function.

The output of the preceding program is shown in Figure 6.7.

FIGURE 6.7

Initialing a two-dimensional array with nested loops.

Looping through two-dimensional arrays with nested loops can certainly be a daunting task for the beginning programmer. My best advice is to practice, practice, and practice! The more you program, the clearer the concepts will become.

Searching Two-Dimensional Arrays

The concept behind searching a two-dimensional array is similar to that of searching a single-dimension array. You must receive a searchable value, such as user input, and then search the array's contents until a value is found or the entire array has been searched without a match.

When searching two-dimensional arrays, however, you must use the nested looping techniques I described in the previous section. The nested looping constructs allow you to search each array element individually.

The following program demonstrates how to search a two-dimensional array.

```
#include <stdio.h>

main()

{

    int iTwoD[3][3] = { {1, 2, 3}, {4, 5, 6}, {7, 8, 9} };
    int iFoundAt[2] = {0, 0};

    int x, y;
    int iValue = 0;
    int iFound = 0;

    printf("\nEnter your search value: ");
    scanf("%d", &iValue);

    //search the 2-D array
    for ( x = 0; x <= 2; x++ ) {

        for ( y = 0; y <= 2; y++ ) {

            if ( iTwoD[x][y] == iValue ) {
```

```
            iFound = 1;
            iFoundAt[0] = x;
            iFoundAt[1] = y;
            break;

        }  //end if

    }  //end inner loop

} //end outer loop

if ( iFound == 1 )
    printf("\nFound value in iTwoD[%d][%d]\n", iFoundAt[0], iFoundAt[1]);
else
    printf("\nValue not found\n");

} //end main
```

The architecture of the preceding nested looping structure is a reoccurring theme when dealing with two-dimensional arrays. More specifically, you must use two loops to search a two-dimensional array: one loop to search the rows and an inner loop to search each column for the outer loop's row.

In addition to using the multidimensional array, I use a single-dimension array, called iFoundAt, to store the row and column location of the two-dimensional array if the search value is found. If the search value is found, I want to let the user know where his value was found.

The output of the searchable two-dimensional array program is shown in Figure 6.8.

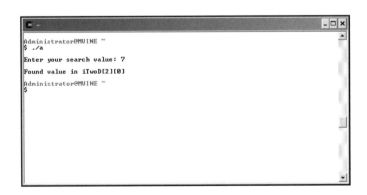

FIGURE 6.8

Searching a two-dimensional array with nested loops.

Chapter Program—Tic-Tac-Toe

The tic-tac-toe game, as shown in Figure 6.9, is a fun and easy way to demonstrate the techniques and array data structures you learned about in this chapter. Moreover, the tic-tac-toe game uses techniques and programming structures that you learned in previous chapters, such as function prototypes, definitions, system calls, and global variables.

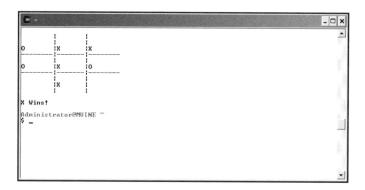

Figure 6.9

Tic-tac-toe as the chapter-based game.

There are a total of four functions, including the `main()` function, that are used to build the tic-tac-toe game. Table 6.3 describes each function's purpose.

TABLE 6.3 FUNCTIONS USED IN THE TIC-TAC-TOE GAME	
Function Name	**Function Description**
`main()`	Initializes array and prompt players for X and O placement until the game is over
`displayBoard()`	Clears the screen and displays the board with X and O placements
`verifySelection()`	Verifies square is empty before placing an X or O inside the square
`checkForWin()`	Checks for a win by X or O or a tie (cat) game

All of the code required to build the tic-tac-toe game is shown next.

```
#include <stdio.h>

/********************************
function prototypes
********************************/
void displayBoard();
```

```
int verifySelection(int, int);
void checkForWin();

/******************
global variables
******************/
char board[8];
char cWhoWon = ' ';
int iCurrentPlayer = 0;


/*********************************************************
begin main function
*********************************************************/
main()  {

   int x;
   int iSquareNum = 0;

   for ( x = 0; x < 9; x++ )
      board[x] = ' ';

   displayBoard();

   while ( cWhoWon == ' ') {

      printf("\n%c\n", cWhoWon);

      if ( iCurrentPlayer == 1 || iCurrentPlayer == 0 ) {

         printf("\nPLAYER X\n");
         printf("Enter an available square number (1-9): ");
         scanf("%d", &iSquareNum);

         if ( verifySelection(iSquareNum, iCurrentPlayer) == 1 )
            iCurrentPlayer = 1;
         else
            iCurrentPlayer = 2;
```

```
        }

        else {

            printf("\nPLAYER O\n");
            printf("Enter an available square number (1-9): ");
            scanf("%d", &iSquareNum);

            if ( verifySelection(iSquareNum, iCurrentPlayer) == 1 )
                iCurrentPlayer = 2;
            else
                iCurrentPlayer = 1;

        }  // end if

        displayBoard();
        checkForWin();

    }  //end loop

}  //end main function

/************************************************************
begin function definition
************************************************************/
void displayBoard() {

    system("clear");
    printf("\n\t|\t|\n");
    printf("\t|\t|\n");
    printf("%c\t|%c\t|%c\n", board[0], board[1], board[2]);
    printf("--------|-------|--------\n");
    printf("\t|\t|\n");
    printf("%c\t|%c\t|%c\n", board[3], board[4], board[5]);
    printf("--------|-------|--------\n");
    printf("\t|\t|\n");
    printf("%c\t|%c\t|%c\n", board[6], board[7], board[8]);
    printf("\t|\t|\n");
```

```
}  //end function definition


/**********************************************************
begin function definition
**********************************************************/
int verifySelection(int iSquare, int iPlayer) {

    if ( board[iSquare - 1] == ' ' && (iPlayer == 1 || iPlayer == 0) ) {
        board[iSquare - 1] = 'X';
        return 0;
    }

    else if ( board[iSquare - 1] == ' ' && iPlayer == 2 ) {
        board[iSquare - 1] = '0';
        return 0;
    }

    else
        return 1;

}   //end function definition


/**********************************************************
begin function definition
**********************************************************/
void checkForWin() {

    int catTotal;
    int x;

    if (board[0] == 'X' && board[1] == 'X' && board[2] == 'X')
        cWhoWon = 'X';
    else if (board[3] == 'X' && board[4] == 'X' && board[5] == 'X')
        cWhoWon = 'X';
    else if (board[6] == 'X' && board[7] == 'X' && board[8] == 'X')
        cWhoWon = 'X';
    else if (board[0] == 'X' && board[3] == 'X' && board[6] == 'X')
        cWhoWon = 'X';
```

```
else if (board[1] == 'X' && board[4] == 'X' && board[7] == 'X')
    cWhoWon = 'X';
else if (board[2] == 'X' && board[5] == 'X' && board[8] == 'X')
    cWhoWon = 'X';
else if (board[0] == 'X' && board[5] == 'X' && board[8] == 'X')
    cWhoWon = 'X';
else if (board[2] == 'X' && board[5] == 'X' && board[6] == 'X')
    cWhoWon = 'X';
else if (board[0] == 'O' && board[1] == 'O' && board[2] == 'O')
    cWhoWon = 'O';
else if (board[3] == 'O' && board[4] == 'O' && board[5] == 'O')
    cWhoWon = 'O';
else if (board[6] == 'O' && board[7] == 'O' && board[8] == 'O')
    cWhoWon = 'O';
else if (board[0] == 'O' && board[3] == 'O' && board[7] == 'O')
    cWhoWon = 'O';
else if (board[1] == 'O' && board[4] == 'O' && board[7] == 'O')
    cWhoWon = 'O';
else if (board[2] == 'O' && board[5] == 'O' && board[8] == 'O')
    cWhoWon = 'O';
else if (board[0] == 'O' && board[5] == 'O' && board[8] == 'O')
    cWhoWon = 'O';
else if (board[2] == 'O' && board[5] == 'O' && board[6] == 'O')
    cWhoWon = 'O';

if (cWhoWon == 'X') {
    printf("\nX Wins!\n");
    return;
}

if (cWhoWon == 'O') {
    printf("\nO Wins!\n");
    return;
}

//check for CAT / draw game
for ( x = 0; x < 9; x++ ) {
    if ( board[x] != ' ')
```

```
        catTotal += 1;

}   //end for loop

if ( catTotal == 9 ) {
    cWhoWon = 'C';
    printf("\nCAT Game!\n");
    return;

}   //end if

} //end function definition
```

SUMMARY

- An array is a grouping of contiguous memory segments.
- Variables in an array share the same name.
- Variables in an array share the same data type.
- Individual variables in an array are called elements.
- Elements in an array are accessed with an index number.
- Assigning the single numeric value of 0 in an array declaration will, by default, assign all array elements the value of 0.
- Elements in a character array hold characters plus a special null termination character, which is represented by the character constant '/0'.
- When creating character arrays, be sure to allocate enough room to store the largest character sequence assignable. Also, remember to allow enough room in the character array for storing the null character ('\0').
- Use looping structures, such as the for loop, to iterate through each element in an array.
- When C encounters the break keyword in a loop, it moves program control to the next statement outside of the loop.
- C implements two-dimensional arrays as single-dimension arrays with pointers to other single-dimension arrays.
- The easiest way to understand or think about two-dimensional arrays is to visualize a table with rows and columns.
- Nested loops are necessary to search through a two-dimensional array.

CHALLENGES

1. Build a program that uses a single-dimension array to store 10 numbers input by a user. After inputting the numbers, the user should see a menu with two options to sort and print the 10 numbers in ascending or descending order.

2. Create a student GPA average calculator. The program should prompt the user to enter up to 30 GPAs, which are stored in a single-dimension array. Each time he or she enters a GPA, the user should have the option to calculate the current GPA average or enter another GPA. Sample data for this program is shown below.

   GPA: 3.5
   GPA: 2.8
   GPA: 3.0
   GPA: 2.5
   GPA: 4.0
   GPA: 3.7
   GPA Average: 3.25

   Hint: Be careful to not calculate empty array elements into your student GPA average.

3. Create a program that allows a user to enter up to five names of friends. Use a two-dimensional array to store the friends' names. After each name is entered, the user should have the option to enter another name or print out a report that shows each name entered thus far.

4. Modify the tic-tac-toe game to use a two-dimensional array instead of a single-dimension array.

5. Modify the tic-tac-toe program or build your own tic-tac-toe game to be a single player game (the user will play against the computer).

POINTERS

No doubts about it, pointers are one of the most challenging topics in C programming. Yet they are what make C one of the most robust languages in the computing industry for building unparalleled efficient and powerful programs.

Pointers are paramount to understanding the remainder of this book, and for that matter, the rest of what C has to offer. Despite their challenges, keep one thing in mind: Every beginning C programmer (including myself) has struggled through pointer concepts. You can think of pointers as a rite-of-passage for any C programmer.

To get started, I will show you the following fundamentals:

- Pointer fundamentals
- Functions and pointers
- Passing arrays to functions
- The const qualifier

After mastering this chapter's concepts, you will be ready to study more sophisticated pointer concepts and their applications, such as strings, dynamic memory allocation, and various data structures.

POINTER FUNDAMENTALS

Pointers are very powerful structures that can be used by C programmers to work with variables, functions, and data structures through their memory addresses. Pointers are variables that most often contain a memory address as their value. In other words, a pointer variable contains a memory address that points to another variable. Huh? That may have sounded weird, so let's discuss an example: Say I have an integer variable called iResult that contains the value 75 with a memory address of 0x948311. Now say I have a pointer variable called myPointer, which does not contain a data value, but instead contains a memory address of 0x948311, which by the way is the same memory address of my integer variable iResult. This means that my pointer variable called myPointer indirectly points to the value of 75. This concept is known as *indirection* and it is an essential pointer concept.

 Believe it or not you have already worked with pointers in Chapter 6. Specifically, an array name is nothing more than a pointer to the start of the array!

Declaring and Initializing Pointer Variables

Pointer variables must be declared before they can be used, as shown in the following code:

```
int x = 0;
int iAge = 30;
int *ptrAge;
```

Simply place the indirection operator (*) in front of the variable name to declare a pointer. In the previous example I declared three variables, two integer variables and one pointer variable. For readability purposes, I use the naming convention ptr as a prefix. This helps me and other programmers identify this variable as a pointer.

 Naming conventions, such as ptr, are not required. Variable names and naming conventions do not matter in C. They simply help you identify the data type of the variable and, if possible, the purpose of the variable.

When I declared the pointer ptrAge, I was telling C that I want my pointer variable to indirectly point to an integer data type. My pointer variable, however, is not pointing to anything just yet. To indirectly reference a value through a pointer, you must assign an address to the pointer, as shown here:

```
ptrAge = &iAge;
```

In this statement, I assign the memory address of the iAge variable to the pointer variable (ptrAge). Indirection in this case is accomplished by placing the unary operator (&) in front of the variable `iAge`. This statement is telling C that I want to assign the memory address of `iAge` to my pointer variable `ptrAge`.

The unary operator (&) is often referred to as the "address of" operator because, in this case, my pointer `ptrAge` is receiving the "address of" `iAge`.

Conversely, I can assign the contents of what my pointer variable points to—a non-pointer data value—as demonstrated next.

```
x = *ptrAge;
```

The variable `x` will now contain the integer value of what `ptrAge` points to—in this case the integer value 30.

To get a better idea of how pointers and indirection work, study Figure 7.1.

```
int x = 0;
int iAge = 30;
int *ptrAge = NULL;
```

Memory information after variable declaration & initialization

```
Name: x              Name: iAge           Name: ptrAge
Address: 0xHH        Address: 0xFF        Address: 0x22
Value: 0             Value: 30            Value: NULL
```

```
int *ptrAge = &iAge;
```

...**ptrAge** is assigned the value (in this case an address) of **iAge**

```
Name: ptrAge
Address: 0x22
Value: 0xFF
```

```
x = *ptrAge;
```

...**x** is assigned the value of what **ptrAge** points to

```
Name: x
Address: 0xHH
Value: 30
```

FIGURE 7.1

A graphical representation of indirection with pointers.

Not initializing your pointer variables can result in invalid data or invalid expression results. Pointer variables should always be initialized with another variable's memory address, with 0, or with the keyword `NULL`. The next code block demonstrates a few valid pointer initializations.

```
int *ptr1;
int *ptr2;
int *ptr3;

ptr1 = &x;
ptr2 = 0;
ptr3 = NULL;
```

Remembering that pointer variables can only be assigned memory addresses, 0, or the NULL value is the first step in learning to work with pointers. Consider the following example, in which I try to assign a non-address value to a pointer.

```
#include <stdio.h>

main()

{

    int x = 5;
    int *iPtr;

    iPtr = 5; //this is wrong
    iPtr = x; //this is also wrong

}
```

You can see that I tried to assign the integer value 5 to my pointer. This type of assignment will cause a compile time error, as shown in Figure 7.2.

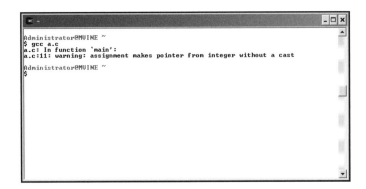

FIGURE 7.2

Assigning non-address values to pointers.

Assigning non-address values, such as numbers or characters, to a pointer without a cast will cause compile time errors.

You can, however, assign non-address values to pointers by using an indirection operator (*), as shown next.

```c
#include <stdio.h>

main()

{

    int x = 5;
    int *iPtr;

    iPtr = &x;  //iPtr is assigned the address of x
    *iPtr = 7;  //the value of x is indirectly changed to 7

}
```

This program assigns the memory address of variable x to the pointer variable (iPtr) and then indirectly assigns the integer value 7 to variable x.

Printing Pointer Variable Contents

To verify indirection concepts, print the memory address of pointers and non-pointer variables using the %p conversion specifier. To demonstrate the %p conversion specifier, study the following program.

```c
#include <stdio.h>

main()

{

    int x = 1;
    int *iPtr;

    iPtr = &x;
```

```
    *iPtr = 5;

    printf("\n*iPtr = %p\n&x = %p\n", iPtr, &x);

}
```

I use the %p conversion specifier to print the memory address for the pointer and integer variable. As shown in Figure 7.3, the pointer variable contains the same memory address (in hexadecimal format) of the integer variable x.

FIGURE 7.3

Printing a memory
address with the
%p conversion
specifier.

The next program (and its output in Figure 7.4) continues to demonstrate indirection concepts and the %p conversion specifier.

```c
#include <stdio.h>

main()

{

    int x = 5;
    int y = 10;
    int *iPtr = NULL;

    printf("\niPtr points to: %p\n", iPtr);

    //assign memory address of y to pointer
    iPtr = &y;
    printf("\niPtr now points to: %p\n", iPtr);
```

```
//change the value of x to the value of y
x = *iPtr;
printf("\nThe value of x is now: %d\n", x);

//change the value of y to 15
*iPtr = 15;
printf("\nThe value of y is now: %d\n", y);

}
```

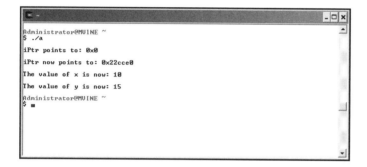

FIGURE 7.4

Using pointers and
assignment
statements to
demonstrate
indirection.

FUNCTIONS AND POINTERS

One of the greatest benefits of using pointers is the ability to pass arguments to functions by reference. By default, arguments are passed by value in C, which involves making a copy of the incoming argument for the function to use. Depending on the storage requirements of the incoming argument, this may not be the most efficient use of memory. To demonstrate, study the following program.

```
#include <stdio.h>

int addTwoNumbers(int, int);

main()

{

    int x = 0;
    int y = 0;
```

```
    printf("\nEnter first number: ");
    scanf("%d", &x);
    printf("\nEnter second number: ");
    scanf("%d", &y);

    printf("\nResult is %d\n", addTwoNumbers(x, y));

}  //end main

int addTwoNumbers(int x, int y)

{

    return x + y;

}  //end addTwoNumbers
```

In this program, I pass two integer arguments to my `addTwoNumbers` function in a `printf()` function. This type of argument passing is called *passing by value*. More specifically, C reserves extra memory space to make a copy of variables x and y and the copies of x and y are then sent to the function as arguments. But what does this mean? Two important concerns come to mind.

First, passing arguments by value is not the most efficient programming means for programming in C. Making copies of two integer variables may not seem like a lot of work, but in the real world, C programmers must strive to minimize memory use as much as possible. Think about embedded circuit design where your memory resources are very limited. In these development situations, making copies of variables for arguments can make a big difference. Even if you are not programming embedded circuits, you can find performance degradation when passing large amounts of data by value (think of arrays or data structures that contain large amounts of information such as employee data).

Second, when C passes arguments by value you are unable to modify the original contents of the incoming parameters. This is because C has made a copy of the original variable and hence only the copy is modified. This can be a good thing and a bad thing. For example, you may not want the receiving function modifying the variable's original contents and in this case passing arguments by value is preferred. Moreover, passing arguments by value is one way programmers can implement information hiding as discussed in Chapter 5, "Structured Programming."

To further demonstrate the concepts of passing arguments by value, study the following program and its output shown in Figure 7.5.

```
Administrator@MUINE ~
$ ./a

Enter a number: 57

The value of x is: 62

The original value of x did not change: 57
Administrator@MUINE ~
$
```

FIGURE 7.5

Implementing information hiding by passing arguments by value.

```c
#include <stdio.h>

void demoPassByValue(int);

main()

{

    int x = 0;

    printf("\nEnter a number: ");
    scanf("%d", &x);

    demoPassByValue(x);

    printf("\nThe original value of x did not change: %d\n", x);

}   //end main

void demoPassByValue(int x)

{

    x += 5;
```

```
   printf("\nThe value of x is: %d\n", x);

}   //end demoPassByValue
```

After studying the code, you can see that I attempt to modify the incoming parameter by incrementing it by five. The argument appears to be modified when I print the contents in the demoPassByValue's printf() function. However, when I print the contents of variable x from the main() function, it indeed is not modified.

To solve this problem, you use pointers to pass arguments *by reference*. More specifically, you can pass the address of the variable (argument) to the function using indirection, as demonstrated in the next program and in Figure 7.6.

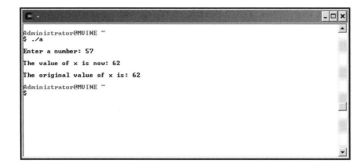

FIGURE 7.6

Passing an argument by reference using indirection.

```
#include <stdio.h>

void demoPassByReference(int *);

main()

{

    int x = 0;

    printf("\nEnter a number: ");
    scanf("%d", &x);

    demoPassByReference(&x);

    printf("\nThe original value of x is: %d\n", x);
```

```
}   //end main

void demoPassByReference(int *ptrX)

{

    *ptrX += 5;

    printf("\nThe value of x is now: %d\n", *ptrX);

}   //end demoPassByReference
```

To pass arguments by reference, you need to be aware of a few subtle differences in the preceding program. The first noticeable difference is in the function prototype, as shown next.

```
void demoPassByReference(int *);
```

I tell C that my function will take a pointer as an argument by placing the indirection (*) operator after the data type. The next slight difference is in my function call, to which I pass the memory address of the variable x by placing the unary (&) operator in front of the variable, as demonstrated next.

```
demoPassByReference(&x);
```

The rest of the pertinent indirection activities are performed in the function implementation where I tell the function header to expect an incoming parameter (pointer) that points to an integer value. This is known as passing by reference!

```
void demoPassByReference(int *ptrX)
```

To modify the original contents of the argument, I must again use the indirection operator (*), which tells C that I want to access the contents of the memory location contained in the pointer variable. Specifically, I increment the original variable contents by five, as shown next.

```
*ptrX += 5;
```

I use the indirection operator in a `printf()` function to print the pointer's contents.

```
printf("\nThe value of x is now: %d\n", *ptrX);
```

CAUTION If you forget to place the indirection (*) operator in front of a pointer in a print statement that displays a number with the %d conversion specifier, C will print a numeric representation of the pointer address.

```
printf("\nThe value of x is now: %d\n", ptrX);    //this is wrong
printf("\nThe value of x is now: %d\n", *ptrX); //this is right
```

Up to now, you may have been wondering why it is necessary to place an ampersand (also known as the "address of" operator) in front of variables in scanf() functions. Quite simply, the address operator provides the scanf() function the memory address to which C should write data typed in from the user.

PASSING ARRAYS TO FUNCTIONS

You may remember from Chapter 6, "Arrays," that arrays are groupings of contiguous memory segments and that the array name itself is a pointer to the first memory location in the contiguous memory segment. Arrays and pointers are closely related in C. In fact, passing an array name to a pointer assigns the first memory location of the array to the pointer variable. To demonstrate this concept, the next program creates and initializes an array of five elements and declares a pointer that is initialized to the array name. Initializing a pointer to an array name stores the first address of the array in the pointer, which is shown in Figure 7.7.

After initializing the pointer, I can access the first memory address of the array and the array's first element.

```
#include <stdio.h>

main()

{

    int iArray[5] = {1,2,3,4,5};

    int *iPtr = iArray;

    printf("\nAddress of pointer: %p\n", iPtr);
    printf("First address of array: %p\n", &iArray[0]);

    printf("\nPointer points to: %d\n", *iPtr);
```

```
printf("First element of array contains: %d\n", iArray[0]);
```

```
}
```

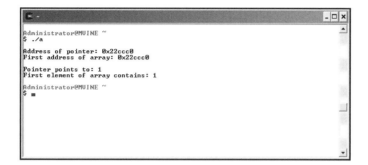

FIGURE 7.7

Assigning the first
address of an array
to a pointer.

Knowing that an array name contains a memory address that points to the first element in the array, you can surmise that array names can be treated much like a pointer when passing arrays to functions. It is not necessary to deal with unary (&) or indirection (*) operators when passing arrays to functions, however. More importantly, arrays passed as arguments are passed by reference automatically. That's an important concept so I'll state it again. *Arrays passed as arguments are passed by reference.*

To pass an array to a function, you need to define your function prototype and definition so that they expect to receive an array as an argument. The next program and its output in Figure 7.8 demonstrate this concept by passing a character array to a function that calculates the length of the incoming string (character array).

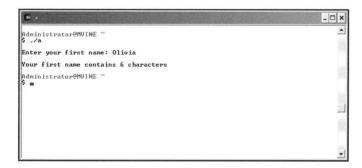

FIGURE 7.8

Passing an array as
an argument.

```
#include <stdio.h>
```

```
int nameLength(char []);
```

```
main()

{

    char aName[20] = {'\0'};

    printf("\nEnter your first name: ");
    scanf("%s", aName);

    printf("\nYour first name contains ");
    printf("%d characters\n", nameLength(aName));

}  //end main

int nameLength(char name[])

{

    int x = 0;

    while ( name[x] != '\0' )
        x++;

    return x;

}  //end nameLength
```

You can build your function prototype to receive an array as an argument by placing empty brackets in the argument list as shown again next.

```
int nameLength(char []);
```

This function prototype tells C to expect an array as an argument and, more specifically, the function will receive the first memory address in the array. When calling the function, I need only to pass the array name as shown in the next print statement.

```
printf("%d characters\n", nameLength(aName));
```

Also notice in the preceding program that I did not use the address of (&) operator in front of the array name in the scanf() function. This is because an array name in C already contains a memory address, which is the address of the first element in the array.

This program is a good demonstration of passing arrays as arguments, but it doesn't serve well to prove arrays are passed by reference. To do so, study the following program and its output in Figure 7.9, which modifies array contents using pass by reference techniques.

FIGURE 7.9

Modifying array contents through indirection and passing arrays to functions.

```
#include <stdio.h>

void squareNumbers(int []);

main()

{

    int x;
    int iNumbers[3] = {2, 4, 6};

    printf("\nThe current array values are: ");

    for ( x = 0; x < 3; x++ )
        printf("%d ", iNumbers[x]); //print contents of array

    printf("\n");

    squareNumbers(iNumbers);

    printf("\nThe modified array values are: ");

    for ( x = 0; x < 3; x++ )
        printf("%d ", iNumbers[x]); //print modified array contents
```

```
   printf("\n");

}  //end main

void squareNumbers(int num[])

{

   int x;

   for ( x = 0; x < 3; x++ )
      num[x] = num[x] * num[x]; //modify the array contents

}  //end squareNumbers
```

THE CONST QUALIFIER

You are now aware that arguments can be passed to functions in one of two ways: pass by value and pass by reference. When passing arguments by value, C makes a copy of the argument for the receiving function to use. Also known as information hiding, this prevents the direct changing of the incoming argument's contents, but it creates additional overhead when passing large structures to functions. Passing arguments by reference, however, provides C programmers the capability of modifying argument contents via pointers.

There are times, however, when you will want the power and speed of passing arguments by reference without the security risk of changing a variable's (argument) contents. C programmers can accomplish this with the const qualifier.

You may remember from Chapter 2, "Primary Data Types," that the const qualifier allows you to create read-only variables. You can also use the const qualifier in conjunction with pointers to achieve a read-only argument while still achieving the pass by reference capability. To demonstrate, the next program passes a read-only integer type argument to a function.

```
#include <stdio.h>

void printArgument(const int *);

main()

{
```

```
    int iNumber = 5;

    printArgument(&iNumber); //pass read-only argument

}  //end main

void printArgument(const int *num) //pass by reference, but read-only

{

    printf("\nRead Only Argument is: %d ", *num);

}
```

Remembering that arrays are passed to functions by reference, you should know that function implementations can alter the original array's contents. To prevent an array argument from being altered in a function, use the const qualifier as demonstrated in the next program.

```
#include <stdio.h>

void printArray(const int []);

main()

{

    int iNumbers[3] = {2, 4, 6};

    printArray(iNumbers);

}  //end main

void printArray(const int num[]) //pass by reference, but read-only

{

    int x;

    printf("\nArray contents are: ");
```

```
    for ( x = 0; x < 3; x++ )
        printf("%d ", num[x]);

}
```

As shown in the preceding program, you can pass an array to a function as read-only by using the const qualifier. To do so, you must tell the function prototype and function definition that it should expect a read-only argument by using the const keyword.

To prove the read-only concept, consider the next program, which attempts to modify the read-only argument in an assignment statement from within the function.

```c
#include <stdio.h>

void modifyArray(const int []);

main()

{

    int iNumbers[3] = {2, 4, 6};

    modifyArray(iNumbers);

}   //end main

void modifyArray(const int num[])

{

    int x;

    for ( x = 0; x < 3; x++ )
        num[x] = num[x] * num[x]; //this will not work!

}
```

Notice the output in Figure 7.10. The C compiler warns me with an error that I'm attempting to modify a read-only location.

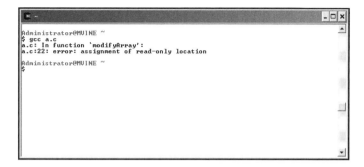

In summary, the `const` qualifier is a very nice solution for securing argument contents in a pass by reference environment.

CHAPTER PROGRAM—CRYPTOGRAM

As revealed in Figure 7.11, the chapter-based program Cryptogram uses many of the techniques you have learned thus far about pointers, arrays, and functions. Before proceeding directly to the program code, however, the next section will give you some basic information on cryptograms and encryption that will assist you in understanding the chapter-based program's intent and application.

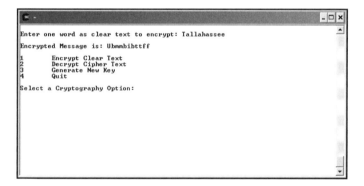

FIGURE 7.11

The chapter-based program, Cryptogram, passes arrays to functions to encrypt and decrypt a word.

Introduction to Encryption

Encryption is a subset of technologies and sciences under the cryptography umbrella. Like the world of computer programming, cryptography and encryption have many specialized keywords, definitions, and techniques. It is prudent to list some of the more common definitions in this section before continuing.

- Cryptography—The art and science of protecting or obscuring messages.
- Cipher text—A message obscured by applying an encryption algorithm.
- Clear text—Plain text or a message readable by humans.
- Cryptogram—An encrypted or protected message.
- Cryptographer—A person or specialist who practices encrypting or protecting messages.
- Encryption—The process by which clear text is converted into cipher text.
- Decryption—The process of converting cipher text into clear text; generally involves knowing a key or formula.
- Key—The formula used to decrypt an encrypted message.

Encryption techniques have been applied for hundreds of years, although it wasn't until the advent of the Internet and the computer age that encryption has gained a level of unprecedented public attention.

Whether it's protecting your credit card information with "dot com" purchases or keeping your personal data on your home PC safe and secure, computing provides a new level of anxiety for everyone.

Fortunately, there are a number of "good guys" out there trying to figure out the right mixture of computer science, math, and cryptography to build safe systems for private and sensitive data. These "good guys" are generally computer companies and computing professionals who attempt to alleviate our anxiety through the promise of intangible or at least unreadable data using encryption.

In a simplified manner, encryption uses many techniques for converting human-readable messages, known as clear text, into an unreadable or obscure message called cipher text. Encrypted messages are generally locked and unlocked with the same key or algorithm. Keys used to lock and unlock secured messages, or cryptograms, can either be stored in the encrypted message itself or be used in conjunction with outside sources, such as account numbers and passwords.

The first step in encrypting any message is to create an encryption algorithm. An oversimplified encryption algorithm discussed in this section is the technique or algorithm called *shift by n*, which changes the shape or meaning of a message. The shift by n algorithm basically says to move each character up or down a scale by a certain number of increments. For example, I can encrypt the following message by shifting each character by two letters.

```
Meet me at seven
```

Shifting each character by two letters produces the following result.

```
Oggv og cv ugxgp
```

The key in the shift by n algorithm is the number used in shifting (the *n* in shift by n). Without this key, it is difficult to decipher or decrypt the encrypted message. It's really quite simple! Of course, this is not an encryption algorithm that the CIA would use to pass data to and from its agents, but you get the point.

The encryption algorithm is only as good as its key is safe. To demonstrate, consider that your house is locked and safe until an unauthorized person gains physical access to your key. Even though you have the best locks money can buy, they no longer provide security because an unwanted person has the key to unlock your house.

As you will see in the next section, you can build your own simple encryption processes with encryption algorithms and encryption keys using C, the ASCII character set, and the shift by n algorithm.

Building the Cryptogram Program

Using your knowledge of beginning encryption concepts, you can easily build an encryption program in C that uses the shift by n algorithm to generate a key and encrypt and decrypt a message.

As shown in Figure 7.11, the user is presented with an option to encrypt a message, decrypt a message, or generate a new key. When a new key is generated, the encryption algorithm uses the new key to shift each letter of the message by *n*, in which *n* is the random number generated by selecting the "generate new key" option. The same key is again used to decrypt the message.

If you generate a new key after encrypting a message, it is quite possible that you will be unable to decrypt the previously encrypted message. This demonstrates the importance of knowing the encryption key on both ends of the cryptogram.

All of the code needed to build the Cryptogram program is shown next.

```c
#include <stdio.h>
#include <stdlib.h>

//function prototypes
void encrypt(char [], int);
void decrypt(char [], int);
```

```c
main()

{

    char myString[21] = {0};
    int iSelection = 0;
    int iRand;

    srand(time(NULL));

    iRand = (rand() % 4) + 1; // random #, 1-4

    while ( iSelection != 4 ) {

        printf("\n\n1\tEncrypt Clear Text\n");
        printf("2\tDecrypt Cipher Text\n");
        printf("3\tGenerate New Key\n");
        printf("4\tQuit\n");
        printf("\nSelect a Cryptography Option: ");
        scanf("%d", &iSelection);

        switch (iSelection) {

        case 1:
            printf("\nEnter one word as clear text to encrypt: ");
            scanf("%s", myString);
            encrypt(myString, iRand);
            break;

        case 2:
            printf("\nEnter cipher text to decrypt: ");
            scanf("%s", myString);
            decrypt(myString, iRand);
            break;

        case 3:
            iRand = (rand() % 4) + 1; // random #, 1-4
            printf("\nNew Key Generated\n");
```

```
      break;

   }  //end switch

   }  //end loop

}  //end main

void encrypt(char sMessage[], int random)

{

   int x = 0;

//encrypt the message by shifting each characters ASCII value
   while ( sMessage[x] ) {
      sMessage[x] += random;
      x++;

   } //end loop

   x = 0;
   printf("\nEncrypted Message is: ");

//print the encrypted message
   while ( sMessage[x] ) {
      printf("%c", sMessage[x]);
      x++;

   } //end loop

}  //end encrypt function

void decrypt(char sMessage[], int random)

{

   int x = 0;
```

```
    x = 0;

//decrypt the message by shifting each characters ASCII value
    while ( sMessage[x] ) {
        sMessage[x] = sMessage[x] - random;
        x++;

    } //end loop

    x = 0;
    printf("\nDecrypted Message is: ");

//print the decrypted message
    while ( sMessage[x] ) {
        printf("%c", sMessage[x]);
        x++;

    } //end loop

}   //end decrypt function
```

SUMMARY

- Pointers are variables that contain a memory address that points to another variable.
- Place the indirection operator (*) in front of the variable name to declare a pointer.
- The unary operator (&) is often referred to as the "address of" operator.
- Pointer variables should always be initialized with another variable's memory address, with 0, or with the keyword NULL.
- You can print the memory address of pointers using the %p conversion specifier.
- By default, arguments are passed by value in C, which involves making a copy of the incoming argument for the function to use.
- Pointers can be used to pass arguments by reference.
- Passing an array name to a pointer assigns the first memory location of the array to the pointer variable. Similarly, initializing a pointer to an array name stores the first address of the array in the pointer.
- You can use the const qualifier in conjunction with pointers to achieve a read-only argument while still achieving the pass by reference capability.

CHALLENGES

1. Build a program that performs the following operations:

   - Declares three pointer variables called iPtr of type int, cPtr of type char, and fFloat of type float.
   - Declares three new variables called iNumber of int type, fNumber of float type, and cCharacter of char type.
   - Assigns the address of each non-pointer variable to the matching pointer variable.
   - Prints the value of each non-pointer variable.
   - Prints the value of each pointer variable.
   - Prints the address of each non-pointer variable.
   - Prints the address of each pointer variable.

2. Create a program that allows a user to select one of the following four menu options:

   - Enter New Integer Value
   - Print Pointer Address
   - Print Integer Address
   - Print Integer Value

   For this program you will need to create two variables: one integer data type and one pointer. Using indirection, assign any new integer value entered by the user through an appropriate pointer.

3. Create a dice rolling game. The game should allow a user to toss up to six dice at a time. Each toss of a die will be stored in a six-element integer array. The array will be created in the main() function, but passed to a new function called TossDie(). The TossDie() function will take care of generating random numbers from one to six and assigning them to the appropriate array element number.

4. Modify the Cryptogram program to use a different type of key system or algorithm. Consider using a user-defined key or a different character set.

STRINGS

Strings use many concepts you have already learned about in this book, such as functions, arrays, and pointers. This chapter shows you how to build and use strings in your C programs while also outlining the intimate relationships strings have with pointers and arrays. You will also learn many new common library functions for manipulating, converting, and searching strings, as well as the following:

- Reading and printing strings
- String arrays
- Converting strings to numbers
- Manipulating strings
- Analyzing strings

INTRODUCTION TO STRINGS

Strings are groupings of letters, numbers, and many other characters. C programmers can create and initialize a string using a character array and a terminating NULL character, as shown next.

```
char myString[5] = {'M', 'i', 'k', 'e', '\0'};
```

Figure 8.1 depicts this declared array of characters.

CAUTION When creating character arrays, it is important to allocate enough room for the NULL character because many C library functions look for the NULL character when processing character arrays. If the NULL character is not found, some C library functions may not produce the desired result.

FIGURE 8.1

Depicting an array of characters.

The variable `myString` can also be created and initialized with a *string literal*. String literals are groupings of characters enclosed in quotation marks, as shown next.

```
char myString[] = "Mike";
```

Assigning a string literal to a character array, as the preceding code shows, creates the necessary number of memory elements—in this case five including the NULL character.

 TIP *String literals* are a series of characters surrounded by double quotes.

You know that strings are arrays of characters in a logical sense, but it's just as important to know that strings are implemented as a pointer to a segment of memory. More specifically, string names are really just pointers that point to the first character's memory address in a string.

To demonstrate this thought, consider the following program statement.

```
char *myString = "Mike";
```

This statement declares a pointer variable and assigns the string literal "Mike" to the first and subsequent memory locations that the pointer variable `myString` points to. In other words, the pointer variable `myString` points to the first character in the string "Mike".

To further demonstrate this concept, study the following program and its output in Figure 8.2, which reveals how strings can be referenced through pointers and traversed similar to arrays.

```c
#include <stdio.h>

main()

{

    char *myString = "Mike";
    int x;

    printf("\nThe pointer variable's value is: %p\n", *myString);
    printf("\nThe pointer variable points to: %s\n", myString);
    printf("\nThe memory locations for each character are: \n\n");

    //access & print each memory address in hexadecimal format
    for ( x = 0; x < 5; x++ )
        printf("%p\n", myString[x]);

}  //end main
```

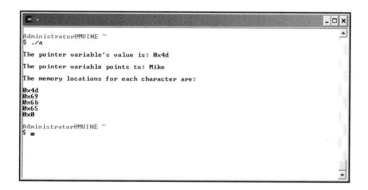

FIGURE 8.2

Creating, manipulating, and printing strings with pointers and arrays of characters.

ARE STRINGS DATA TYPES?

The concept of a string is sometimes taken for granted in high-level languages such as Visual Basic. This is because many high-level languages implement strings as a data type, just like an integer or double. In fact, you may be thinking—or at least hoping—that C contains a string data type as shown next.

```
str myString = "Mike";   //not possible, no such data type
string myString = "Mike";   //not possible, no such data type
```

C does not identify strings as a data type; rather C strings are simply character arrays.

Figure 8.3 further depicts the notion of strings as pointers.

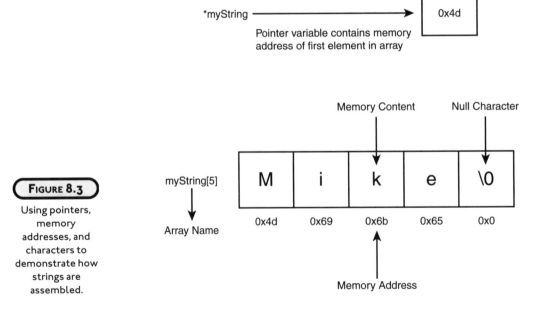

FIGURE 8.3

Using pointers, memory addresses, and characters to demonstrate how strings are assembled.

After studying the preceding program and Figure 8.3, you can see how the pointer variable myString contains the value of a memory address (printed in hexadecimal format) that points to the first character in the string "Mike", followed by subsequent characters and finally the NULL zero to indicate the end of the string.

In the next few sections, you will continue your investigation into strings and their use by learning how to handle string I/O and how to convert, manipulate, and search strings using a few old and new C libraries and their associated functions.

READING AND PRINTING STRINGS

Chapter 6, "Arrays," provided you with an overview of how to read and print array contents. To read and print a character array use the %s conversion specifier as demonstrated in the next program.

```
#include <stdio.h>

main()

{

    char color[12] = {'\0'};

    printf("Enter your favorite color: ");
    scanf("%s", color);

    printf("\nYou entered: %s", color);

}   //end main
```

The preceding program demonstrates reading a string into a character array with initialized and allocated memory (char color[12] = {'\0'};), but what about reading strings from standard input for which you do not know the string length? This is often overlooked in many C texts. It might be natural to assume you can use the standard library's scanf() function, as demonstrated next, to capture and assign string data from standard input to a variable.

```
#include <stdio.h>

main()

{

    char *color;

    printf("\nEnter your favorite color: ");
```

```
scanf("%s", color);   //this will NOT work!

printf("\nYou entered: %s", color);

}  //end main
```

Unfortunately, this program will not work; it will compile, but it will not work. Figure 8.4 demonstrates the inevitable outcome of running the preceding program.

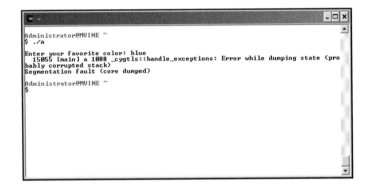

FIGURE 8.4

Reading a string from standard input without allocating memory.

This problem occurs because not only must you declare a string as a pointer to a character, but you must also allocate memory for it. Remember that when first created, a string is nothing more than a pointer that points to nothing valid. Moreover, when the scanf() function attempts to assign data to the pointer's location, the program crashes because memory has not been properly allocated.

For now, you should simply use initialized character arrays with sufficient memory allocated to read strings from standard input. In Chapter 10, "Dynamic Memory Allocation," I will discuss the secret to assigning data from standard input to strings (pointer variables).

STRING ARRAYS

Now you know strings are pointers and that strings, in an abstract sense, are arrays of characters. So, if you need an array of strings, do you need a two-dimensional array or a single-dimension array? The correct answer is both. You can create an array of strings with a one-dimensional pointer array and assign string literals to it or you can create a two-dimensional pointer array, allowing C to reserve enough memory for each character array.

To demonstrate how an array of strings can be created using a single-dimension pointer array of type char, study the following program and its output shown in Figure 8.5.

```
#include <stdio.h>

main()

{

    char *strNames[5] = {0};
    char answer[80] = {0};

    int x;

    strNames[0] = "Michael";
    strNames[1] = "Sheila";
    strNames[2] = "Spencer";
    strNames[3] = "Hunter";
    strNames[4] = "Kenya";

    printf("\nNames in pointer array of type char:\n\n");

    for ( x = 0; x < 5; x++ )
        printf("%s\n", strNames[x]);

}   //end main
```

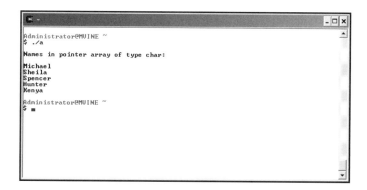

FIGURE 8.5

Printing strings
with a character
pointer array.

In the preceding program, it is very important to note that this array of strings is really an array of character pointers. C is able to treat each element in the array as a string because I used string literals, which C places in protected memory.

Another way to simulate an array of strings is to use a two-dimensional pointer array of type char as seen in the next program.

```
#include <stdio.h>

main()

{

    char *colors[3][10] = {'\0'};

    printf("\nEnter 3 colors seperated by spaces: ");
    scanf("%s %s %s", colors[0], colors[1], colors[2]);

    printf("\nYour entered: ");
    printf("%s %s %s\n", colors[0], colors[1], colors[2]);

}
```

In the preceding program I declared a 3x10 (three by ten) two-dimensional character array that reserves enough memory for 30 characters. Notice I only need to tell C to reference the first dimension of each element in the character array when referencing a single string. Providing I've allocated enough elements in the second dimension, I can easily use scanf() to grab text entered by the user. In Chapter 10, I will show you how to grab portions of contiguous memory without first allocating it in an array.

CONVERTING STRINGS TO NUMBERS

When dealing with ASCII characters, how do you differentiate between numbers and letters? The answer is two-fold. First, programmers assign like characters to various data types, such as characters (char) and integers (int), to differentiate between numbers and letters. This is a straightforward and well-understood approach for differentiating between data types. But there are less defined occasions when programmers will need to convert data from one type to another. For example, there will be times when you will want to convert a string to a number.

Fortunately, the C standard library stdlib.h provides a few functions that serve the purpose of converting strings to numbers. A couple of the most common string conversion functions are shown next.

- atof—Converts a string to a floating-point number
- atoi—Converts a string to an integer

Both of these functions are demonstrated in the next program and the output is shown in Figure 8.6.

```c
#include <stdio.h>
#include <stdlib.h>

main()

{

    char *str1 = "123.79";
    char *str2 = "55";

    float x;
    int y;

    printf("\nString 1 is \"%s\"\n", str1);
    printf("String 2 is \"%s\"\n", str2);

    x = atof(str1);
    y = atoi(str2);

    printf("\nString 1 converted to a float is %.2f\n", x);
    printf("String 2 converted to an integer is %d\n", y);

}   //end main
```

FIGURE 8.6

Converting string literals to numeric types float and int.

When printed to standard output, strings are not surrounded by quotes automatically, as depicted in Figure 8.6. This illusion can be accomplished by using special quote characters in a `printf()` function. You can display quotes in standard output using a conversion specifier, more specifically the `\"` conversion specifier, as the next print statement demonstrates.

```
printf("\nString 1 is \"%s\"\n", str1);
```

You may be wondering why string conversion is so important. Well, for example, attempting numeric arithmetic on strings can produce unexpected results as demonstrated in the next program and in Figure 8.7.

```
#include <stdio.h>

main()

{

    char *str1 = "37";
    char *str2 = "20";

    //produces invalid results
    printf("\nString 1 + String 2 is %d\n", *str1 + *str2);

}   //end main
```

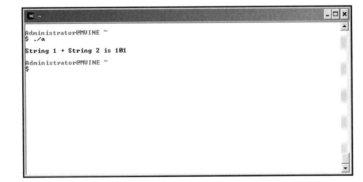

FIGURE 8.7

Invalid arithmetic
results generated
by not converting
strings to
numbers.

In the preceding code, I tried to convert the result using the %d conversion specifier. (%d is the decimal integer conversion specifier.) This is not enough, however, to convert strings or character arrays to numbers, as demonstrated in Figure 8.7.

To correct this problem, you can use string conversion functions, as demonstrated in the next program and its output in Figure 8.8.

```
#include <stdio.h>

main()

{

    char *str1 = "37";
    char *str2 = "20";

    int iResult;

    iResult = atoi(str1) + atoi(str2);

    printf("\nString 1 + String 2 is %d\n", iResult);

}   //end main
```

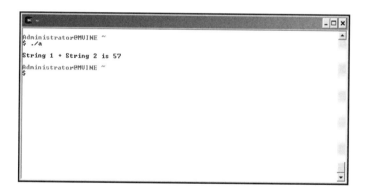

FIGURE 8.8

Using the atoi function to convert strings to numbers.

MANIPULATING STRINGS

A common practice among programmers is manipulating string data, such as copying one string into another and concatenating (gluing) strings to each other. Also common is the need to convert strings to either all lowercase or all uppercase, which can be important when comparing one string to another. I will show you how to perform these string manipulations in the following sections.

strlen()

The string length (strlen()) function is part of the string-handling library <string.h> and is quite simple to understand and use. strlen() takes a reference to a string and returns the numeric string length up to the NULL or terminating character, but not including the NULL character.

The next program and Figure 8.9 demonstrate the strlen() function.

```
#include <stdio.h>
#include <string.h>

main()

{

    char *str1 = "Michael";
    char str2[] = "Vine";

    printf("\nThe length of string 1 is %d\n", strlen(str1));
    printf("The length of string 2 is %d\n", strlen(str2));

}  // end main
```

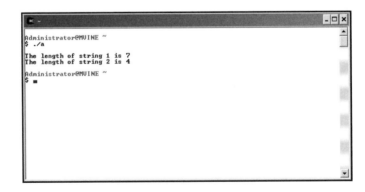

FIGURE 8.9

Using the strlen() function to determine the length of strings.

tolower() and toupper()

An important reason for converting strings to either all uppercase or all lowercase is for string comparisons.

The character-handling library <ctype.h> provides many character manipulation functions such as tolower() and toupper(). These functions provide an easy way to convert a single character to either uppercase or lowercase (notice I said single character). To convert an entire character array to either all uppercase or all lowercase, you will need to work a little harder.

One solution is to build your own user-defined functions for converting character arrays to uppercase or lowercase by looping through each character in the string and using the strlen() function to determine when to stop looping and converting each character to either lower- or uppercase with tolower() and toupper(). This solution is demonstrated in the next program, which uses two user-defined functions and, of course, the character handling functions tolower() and toupper() to convert my first name to all lowercase and my last name to all uppercase. The output is shown in Figure 8.10.

```c
#include <stdio.h>
#include <ctype.h>

//function prototypes
void convertL(char *);
void convertU(char *);

main()

{

    char name1[] = "Michael";
    char name2[] = "Vine";

    convertL(name1);
    convertU(name2);

} //end main

void convertL(char *str)

{

    int x;

    for ( x = 0; x <= strlen(str); x++ )
```

```
            str[x] = tolower(str[x]);

        printf("\nFirst name converted to lower case is %s\n", str);

    } // end convertL

    void convertU(char *str)

    {

        int x;

        for ( x = 0; x <= strlen(str); x++ )
            str[x] = toupper(str[x]);

        printf("Last name converted to upper case is %s\n", str);

    } // end convertU
```

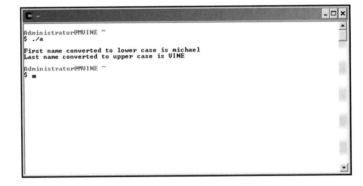

FIGURE 8.10

Manipulating
character arrays
with functions
tolower() and
toupper().

strcpy()

The strcpy() function copies the contents of one string into another string. As you might imagine, it takes two arguments and is pretty straightforward to use, as the next program and Figure 8.11 demonstrate.

```
#include <stdio.h>
#include <string.h>
```

```
main()

{

    char str1[11];
    char *str2 = "C Language";

    printf("\nString 1 now contains %s\n", strcpy(str1, str2));

}  // end main
```

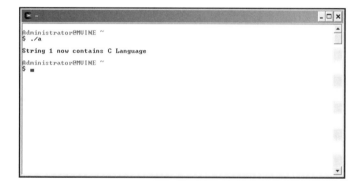

FIGURE 8.11

The output of copying one string to another using the strcpy() function.

The strcpy() function takes two strings as arguments. The first argument is the string to be copied into and the second argument is the string that will be copied from. After copying string 2 (second argument) into string 1 (first argument), the strcpy() function returns the value of string 1.

Note that I declared string 1 (str1) as a character array rather than as a pointer to a char type. Moreover, I gave the character array 11 elements to handle the number characters plus a NULL character. You cannot assign data to an empty string without first allocating memory to it. I'll discuss this more in Chapter 10.

strcat()

Another interesting and sometimes useful string library function is the strcat() function, which concatenates or glues one string to another.

To *concatenate* is to glue one or more pieces of data together or to connect one or more links together.

Like the strcpy() function, the strcat() function takes two string arguments, as the next program demonstrates.

```c
#include <stdio.h>
#include <string.h>

main()

{

    char str1[40] = "Computer Science ";
    char str2[] = "is applied mathematics";

    printf("\n%s\n", strcat(str1, str2));

}  // end main
```

As Figure 8.12 demonstrates, the second string argument (str2) is concatenated to the first string argument (str1). After concatenating the two strings, the strcat() function returns the value in str1. Note that I had to include an extra space at the end of str1 "Computer Science", because the strcat() function does not add a space between the two merged strings.

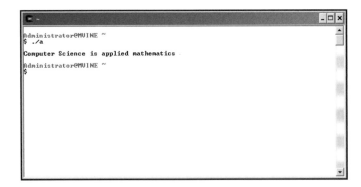

FIGURE 8.12

Using the strcat() function to glue strings together.

ANALYZING STRINGS

In the next couple of sections, I will discuss a few more functions of the string-handling library that allow you to perform various analyses of strings. More specifically, you will learn how to compare two strings for equality and search strings for the occurrence of characters.

strcmp()

The strcmp() function is a very interesting and useful function that is primarily used to compare two strings for equality. Comparing strings is actually a common process for computer and non-computer uses. To demonstrate, consider an old library card-catalog system that used human labor to manually sort book references by various keys (author name, ISBN, title, and so on). Most modern libraries now rely on computer systems and software to automate the process of sorting data for the card catalog system. Keep in mind, the computer does not know that letter A is greater than letter B, or better yet, that the exclamation mark (!) is greater than the letter A. To differentiate between characters, computer systems rely on character codes such as the ASCII character-coding system.

Using character-coding systems, programmers can build sorting software that compares strings (characters). Moreover, C programmers can use built-in string-handling functions, such as strcmp(), to accomplish the same. To prove this, study the following program and its output shown in Figure 8.13.

```
#include <stdio.h>
#include <string.h>

main()

{

    char *str1 = "A";
    char *str2 = "A";
    char *str3 = "!";

    printf("\nstr1 = %s\n", str1);
    printf("\nstr2 = %s\n", str2);
    printf("\nstr3 = %s\n", str3);

    printf("\nstrcmp(str1, str2) = %d\n", strcmp(str1, str2));
    printf("\nstrcmp(str1, str3) = %d\n", strcmp(str1, str3));
    printf("\nstrcmp(str3, str1) = %d\n", strcmp(str3, str1));


    if ( strcmp(str1, str2) == 0 )
       printf("\nLetter A is equal to letter A\n");
```

```
if ( strcmp(str1, str3) > 0 )
   printf("Letter A is greater than character !\n");

if ( strcmp(str3, str1) < 0 )
   printf("Character ! is less than letter A\n");

}   // end main
```

FIGURE 8.13

Comparing strings using the strcmp() function.

The strcmp() function takes two strings as arguments and compares them using corresponding character codes. After comparing the two strings, the strcmp() function returns a single numeric value that indicates whether the first string is equal to, less than, or greater than the second string. Table 8.1 describes the strcmp() function's return values in further detail.

TABLE 8.1   RETURN VALUES AND DESCRIPTIONS FOR THE STRCMP() FUNCTION

Sample Function	Return Value	Description
strcmp(string1, string2)	0	string1 is equal to string2
strcmp(string1, string2)	<0	string1 is less than string2
strcmp(string1, string2)	>0	string1 is greater than string2

strstr()

The strstr() function is a very useful function for analyzing two strings. More specifically, the strstr() function takes two strings as arguments and searches the first string for an occurrence of the second string. This type of search capability is demonstrated in the next program and its output is shown in Figure 8.14.

```c
#include <stdio.h>
#include <string.h>

main()

{

    char *str1 = "Analyzing strings with the strstr() function";
    char *str2 = "ing";
    char *str3 = "xyz";

    printf("\nstr1 = %s\n", str1);
    printf("\nstr2 = %s\n", str2);
    printf("\nstr3 = %s\n", str3);

    if ( strstr(str1, str2) != NULL )
      printf("\nstr2 was found in str1\n");
    else
      printf("\nstr2 was not found in str1\n");

    if ( strstr(str1, str3) != NULL )
      printf("\nstr3 was found in str1\n");
    else
      printf("\nstr3 was not found in str1\n");

} // end main
```

FIGURE 8.14

Using the strstr() function to search one string for another.

As you can see from the preceding program, the strstr() function takes two strings as arguments. The strstr() function looks for the first occurrence of the second argument in the first argument. If the string in the second argument is found in the string in the first argument, the strstr() function returns a pointer to the string in the first argument. Otherwise NULL is returned.

CHAPTER PROGRAM—WORD FIND

The Word Find program is a straightforward program that uses strings and many other chapter-based concepts to create a fun and easy-to-play game. Specifically, it uses concepts and techniques such as arrays and string-based functions that manipulate and analyze strings to build a game. The object of the Word Find game is to challenge a user to find a single word among seemingly meaningless text (see Figure 8.15). All of the code needed to build the Word Find game is shown next.

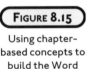

FIGURE 8.15

Using chapter-based concepts to build the Word Find program.

```
#include <stdio.h>
#include <string.h>

//function prototypes
void checkAnswer(char *, char []);

main()

{

char *strGame[5] = {"ADELANGUAGEFERVZOPIBMOU",
                    "ZBPOINTERSKLMLOOPMNOCOT",
                    "PODSTRINGGDIWHIEEICERLS",
```

```
                    "YVCPROGRAMMERWQKNULTHMD",
                    "UKUNIXFIMWXIZEQZINPUTEX"};

char answer[80] = {0};

int displayed = 0;
int x;
int startTime = 0;

system("clear");
printf("\n\n\tWord Find\n\n");

startTime = time(NULL);

for ( x = 0; x < 5; x++ ) {

    /* DISPLAY TEXT FOR A FEW SECONDS */

    while ( startTime + 3 > time(NULL) ) {

        if ( displayed == 0 ) {

            printf("\nFind a word in: \n\n");
            printf("%s\n\n", strGame[x]);
            displayed = 1;

        }   //end if

    }   //end while loop

    system("clear");
    printf("\nEnter word found: ");
    gets(answer);

    checkAnswer(strGame[x], answer);

    displayed = 0;
    startTime = time(NULL);
```

```
}   //end for loop

} //end main


void checkAnswer(char *string1, char string2[])


{

int x;

/* Convert answer to UPPER CASE to perform a valid comparison*/
for ( x = 0; x <= strlen(string2); x++ )
    string2[x] = toupper(string2[x]);


if ( strstr( string1, string2 ) != 0 && string2[0] != 0 )
    printf("\nGreat job!\n");
else
    printf("\nSorry, word not found!\n");

} //end checkAnswer
```

SUMMARY

- Strings are groupings of letters, numbers, and many other characters.
- C programmers can create and initialize a string using a character array and a terminating NULL character.
- Assigning a string literal to a character array creates the necessary number of memory elements including the NULL character.
- String literals are a series of characters surrounded by double quotes.
- You can use the printf() function with the %s conversion specifier to print a string to standard output.
- An array of strings is really an array of character pointers.
- The atof() function converts a string to a floating-point number.
- The atoi() function converts a string to an integer.
- Attempting numeric arithmetic on strings can produce unexpected results.

- The strlen() function takes a reference to a string and returns the numeric string length up to the NULL or terminating character, but not including the NULL character.
- The functions tolower() and toupper() are used to convert a single character to lowercase and uppercase, respectively.
- The strcpy() function copies the contents of one string into another string.
- The strcat() function concatenates or glues one string to another.
- The strcmp() function is used to compare two strings for equality.

CHALLENGES

1. Create a program that performs the following functions:

   - Uses character arrays to read a user's name from standard input.
   - Tells the user how many characters are in his or her name.
   - Displays the user's name in uppercase.

2. Create a program that uses the strstr() function to search the string, "When the going gets tough, the tough stay put!" for the following occurrences (display each occurrence found to standard output):

   - "Going"
   - "tou"
   - "ay put!"

3. Build a program that uses an array of strings to store the following names:

   - "Florida"
   - "Oregon"
   - "California"
   - "Georgia"

   Using the preceding array of strings, write your own sort() function to display each state's name in alphabetical order using the strcmp() function.

4. Modify the Word Find game to include one or more of the following suggestions:

    - Add a menu to the Word Find game that allows the user to select a level of difficulty, such as beginning, intermediate, and advanced. The number of seconds the user has to guess and/or the length of the text in which the user will look for words could determine the level of difficulty.

    - Incorporate multiple words into the text areas.

    - Track the player's score. For example, 1 point for each word guessed correctly and negative 1 point for each word guessed incorrectly.

    - Use the `strlen()` function to ensure the user's input string is the same length as the hidden word.

INTRODUCTION TO DATA STRUCTURES

This chapter introduces a few new computer science concepts for building and using advanced data types (also known as data structures) such as structures and unions, and shows how these user-defined structures assist programmers in defining a more robust, object-aware type. You will learn the differences and similarities between structures and unions and how they relate to real-world computing concepts. In addition to structures, you will learn more about existing data types and how they can be converted from one type to another using type casting. Specifically, this chapter covers the following topics:

- Structures
- Unions
- Type casting

STRUCTURES

Structures are an important computer science concept because they are used throughout the programming and IT world in applications such as relational databases, file-processing, and object-oriented programming concepts. Considered a data type much like an integer or character, structures are more frequently referred to as *data structures*. Structures are found in many high-level languages, including Java, C++, Visual Basic, and, of course, C. When structures are combined with other data types such as pointers, their by-product can be used to build advanced data structures like linked lists, stacks, queues, and trees.

Structures are a collection of variables related in nature, but not necessarily in data type. Structures are most commonly used to define an object—a person, a place, a thing—or similarly a record in a database or file. As you will see next, structures use a few new keywords to build a well-defined collection of variables.

struct

The first process in creating a structure is to build the structure definition using the `struct` keyword followed by braces, with individual variables defined as members. Creating a structure is demonstrated with the following program code:

```
struct math {

    int x;
    int y;
    int result;

};
```

The preceding program statements create a structure definition called `math` that contains three integer-type members. The keyword `math` is also known as the structure tag, which is used to create instances of the structure.

 Members of structures are the individual elements or variables that make up a collection of variables.

 Structure tags identify the structure and can be used to create instances of the structure.

When structure definitions are created using the `struct` keyword, memory is not allocated for the structure until an instance of the structure is created, as demonstrated next.

```
struct math aProblem;
```

The preceding statement uses the `struct` keyword and the structure tag (`math`) to create an instance called `aProblem`. Creating an instance of a structure is really just creating a variable, in this case a variable of structure type.

You can initialize a structure instance the same way you would initialize an array. As demonstrated next, I will supply an initialization list surrounded by braces with each item separated by commas.

```
struct math aProblem = { 0, 0, 0};
```

Only after an instance of the structure has been created can members of the structure be accessed via the dot operator (.), also known as dot notation, as demonstrated next.

```
//assign values to members
aProblem.x = 10;
aProblem.y = 10;
aProblem.result = 20;

//print the contents of aProblem
printf("\n%d plus %d", aProblem.x, aProblem.y);
printf(" equals %d\n", aProblem.result);
```

Notice that members of structures are not required to have the same data type, as shown in the following program.

```
#include <stdio.h>
#include <string.h>

struct employee {

    char fname[10];
    char lname[10];
    int id;
    float salary;

};

main()

{

    //create instance of employee structure
    struct employee emp1;

    //assign values to members
```

```
strcpy(emp1.fname, "Michael");
strcpy(emp1.lname, "Vine");
emp1.id = 123;
emp1.salary = 50000.00;

//print member contents
printf("\nFirst Name: %s\n", emp1.fname);
printf("Last Name: %s\n", emp1.lname);
printf("Employee ID: %d\n", emp1.id);
printf("Salary: $%.2f\n", emp1.salary);

}   //end main
```

Figure 9.1 displays the output of the preceding program.

FIGURE 9.1

Structures with members of different data types.

typedef

The typedef keyword is used for creating structure definitions to build an alias relationship with the structure tag (structure name). It provides a shortcut for programmers when creating instances of the structure. To demonstrate the concept of typedef, I reused the program from the preceding section and modified it to include the typedef alias, as shown next.

```
#include <stdio.h>
#include <string.h>

typedef struct employee {   //modification here

    char fname[10];
    char lname[10];
```

```
    int id;
    float salary;

} emp;   //modification here


main()


{


    //create instance of employee structure using emp
    emp emp1; //modification here

    //assign values to members
    strcpy(emp1.fname, "Michael");
    strcpy(emp1.lname, "Vine");
    emp1.id = 123;
    emp1.salary = 50000.00;

    //print member contents
    printf("\nFirst Name: %s\n", emp1.fname);
    printf("Last Name: %s\n", emp1.lname);
    printf("Employee ID: %d\n", emp1.id);
    printf("Salary: $%.2f\n", emp1.salary);

}   //end main
```

To create a structure alias using `typedef`, I needed to make minimal changes to my program, specifically, the structure definition, as revealed next.

```
typedef struct employee {

    char fname[10];
    char lname[10];
    int id;
    float salary;

} emp;
```

I included the `typedef` keyword in the first line of my structure definition. The next modification is at the end of the structure definition where I tell C that I will use the name `emp` as my alias for the employee structure. Therefore, I no longer have to use the `struct` keyword when creating instances of the employee structure. Instead I can now create instances of my employee structure using the `emp` name just as I would when declaring a variable using standard data types such as `int`, `char`, or `double`. In other words, I now have a data type called `emp`! The next set of program statements demonstrates this concept.

```
emp emp1; // I can now do this
struct employee emp1;  // Instead of doing this
```

To create instances of the employee structure using aliases, supply the alias name followed by a new variable name.

Arrays of Structures

The process for creating and working with an array of structures is very similar to working with arrays containing other data types, such as integers, characters, or floats.

APPLIED STRUCTURES

If you are familiar with database concepts, you can think of a single structure as one database record. To demonstrate, consider an employee structure that contains members (attributes) of an employee, such as name, employee ID, hire-date, salary, and so on. Moreover, if a single instance of an employee structure represents one employee database record, then an array of employee structures is equivalent to, say, a database table containing multiple employee records.

To create an array of structures, supply the desired number of array elements surrounded by brackets after the structure definition, as shown next.

```
typedef struct employee {

    char fname[10];
    char lname[10];
    int id;
    float salary;
```

```
} emp;
```

```
emp emp1[5];
```

To access individual elements in a structure array, you need to provide the array element number surrounded by brackets. To access individual structure members, you need to supply the dot operator followed by the structure member name, as revealed in the next segment of code, which uses the strcpy() function to copy the text "Spencer" into the memory reserved by the structure member.

```
strcpy(emp1[0].fname, "Spencer");
```

The next program and its output, shown in Figure 9.2, demonstrate arrays of structures in more detail.

```
#include <stdio.h>
#include <string.h>

typedef struct scores {

    char name[10];
    int score;

} s;

main()

{

    s highScores[3];
    int x;

    //assign values to members
    strcpy(highScores[0].name, "Hunter");
    highScores[0].score = 40768;

    strcpy(highScores[1].name, "Kenya");
    highScores[1].score = 38565;

    strcpy(highScores[2].name, "Apollo");
```

```
highScores[2].score = 35985;

//print array content
printf("\nTop 3 High Scores\n");

for ( x = 0; x < 3; x++ )
  printf("\n%s\t%d\n", highScores[x].name, highScores[x].score);

} //end main
```

FIGURE 9.2

Creating and using arrays of structures.

PASSING STRUCTURES TO FUNCTIONS

To utilize the power of structures, you need to understand how they are passed to functions for processing. Structures can be passed to functions in a multitude of ways, including passing by value for read-only access and passing by reference for modifying structure member contents.

TIP *Passing by value* protects an incoming variable's value by sending a copy of the original data rather than the actual variable to the function.

TIP *Passing by reference* sends a variable's memory address to a function, which allows statements in the function to modify the original variable's memory contents.

Passing Structures by Value

Like any parameter passed by value, C makes a *copy* of the incoming structure variable for the function to use. Any modifications made to the parameter within the receiving function are not made to the original variable's value. To pass a structure by value to a function, you need only to supply the function prototype and function definition with the structure tag (or the alias if typedef is used). This process is demonstrated in the next program and its corresponding output in Figure 9.3.

```
#include <stdio.h>
#include <string.h>

typedef struct employee {

  int id;
  char name[10];
  float salary;

} e;

void processEmp(e); //supply prototype with structure alias name

main()

{

  e emp1 = {0,0,0}; //Initialize members

  processEmp(emp1); //pass structure by value

  printf("\nID: %d\n", emp1.id);
  printf("Name: %s\n", emp1.name);
  printf("Salary: $%.2f\n", emp1.salary);

} // end main

void processEmp(e emp) //receives a copy of the structure

{

  emp.id = 123;
  strcpy(emp.name, "Sheila");
  emp.salary = 65000.00;

} //end processEmp
```

FIGURE 9.3

Passing a structure by value to a function does not change the original values of the structure's members.

As you can see in Figure 9.3, the structure's members still contain their initialization values even though the structure members appear to be updated in the processEmp() function. The structure's original member contents weren't really modified. In fact, only a copy of the structure's members were accessed and modified. In other words, passing by value causes the processEmp() function to modify a copy of the structure rather than its original member contents.

Passing Structures by Reference

Passing structures by reference requires a bit more knowledge and adherence to C rules and regulations. Before learning how to pass structures by reference, you need to learn a second means for accessing members of structures. In this approach, members can be accessed via the structure pointer operator (->). The structure pointer operator is a dash followed by the greater-than sign with no spaces in between, as demonstrated next.

```
emp->salary = 80000.00;
```

The structure pointer operator is used to access a structure member through a pointer. This form of member access is useful when you have created a pointer of structure type and need to indirectly reference a member's value.

The next program demonstrates how a pointer of structure type is created and its members are accessed via the structure pointer operator.

```
#include <stdio.h>
#include <string.h>

main()

{
```

```
typedef struct player {

char name[15];
float score;

} p;

p aPlayer = {0, 0}; // create instance of structure
p *ptrPlayer; // create a pointer of structure type

ptrPlayer = &aPlayer; // assign address to pointer of structure type

strcpy(ptrPlayer->name, "Pinball Wizard");  // access through indirection
ptrPlayer->score = 1000000.00;

printf("\nPlayer: %s\n", ptrPlayer->name);
printf("Score: %.0f\n", ptrPlayer->score);

} //end main
```

When you understand the structure pointer operator, passing structures by reference is really quite easy. For the most part, structures passed by reference follow the same rules as any other variable passed by reference. Simply tell the function prototype and its definition to expect a pointer of structure type and remember to use the structure pointer operator (->) inside your functions to access each structure member.

To further demonstrate these concepts, study the next program's implementation.

```
#include <stdio.h>
#include <string.h>

typedef struct employee {

  int id;
  char name[10];
  float salary;

} emp;

void processEmp(emp *);
```

```
main()

{

    emp emp1 = {0, 0, 0};
    emp *ptrEmp;

    ptrEmp = &emp1;

    processEmp(ptrEmp);

    printf("\nID: %d\n", ptrEmp->id);
    printf("Name: %s\n", ptrEmp->name);
    printf("Salary: $%.2f\n", ptrEmp->salary);

} // end main

void processEmp(emp *e)

{

    e->id = 123;
    strcpy(e->name, "Sheila");
    e->salary = 65000.00;

} //end processEmp
```

Figure 9.4 demonstrates the output of the previous program and more specifically demonstrates how passing by reference allows functions to modify the original contents of variables, including structure variables.

Passing Arrays of Structures

Unless otherwise specified, passing arrays of structures to functions is automatically passing by reference; it is also known as passing by address. This is true because an array name is really nothing more than a pointer!

FIGURE 9.4

Passing structures
by reference
allows a called
function to modify
the original
contents of the
structure's
members.

To pass an array of structures, simply supply the function prototype with a pointer to the structure, as demonstrated in the next modified program.

```c
#include <stdio.h>
#include <string.h>

typedef struct employee {

    int id;
    char name[10];
    float salary;

} e;

void processEmp( e * ); //supply prototype with pointer of structure type

main()

{

    e emp1[3] = {0,0,0};
    int x;

    processEmp( emp1 ); //pass array name, which is a pointer

    for ( x = 0; x < 3; x++ ) {

        printf("\nID: %d\n", emp1[x].id);
```

```
        printf("Name: %s\n", emp1[x].name);
        printf("Salary: $%.2f\n\n", emp1[x].salary);

    } //end loop

} // end main

void processEmp( e * emp ) //function receives a pointer

{

    emp[0].id = 123;
    strcpy(emp[0].name, "Sheila");
    emp[0].salary = 65000.00;

    emp[1].id = 234;
    strcpy(emp[1].name, "Hunter");
    emp[1].salary = 28000.00;

    emp[2].id = 456;
    strcpy(emp[2].name, "Kenya");
    emp[2].salary = 48000.00;

} //end processEmp
```

As shown in Figure 9.5, the processEmp() function can modify the structure's original member contents using pass by reference techniques.

FIGURE 9.5

Passing an array of structures by reference.

You do not need to use pointers when passing an array of structures to a function because array names *are* pointers! Structure arrays can also be passed by reference simply by telling the function prototype and function definition to receive an array of structure type using empty brackets, as demonstrated next.

```
void processEmp( e [] ); //function prototype

void processEmp( e emp[] ) //function definition
{

}
```

Passing an array to a function is actually passing the first memory address of the array. This type of action produces a simulated pass by reference outcome that allows the user to modify each structure and its members directly.

UNIONS

Although similar to structures in design and use, *unions* provide a more economical way to build objects with attributes (members) that are not required to be in use at the same time. Whereas structures reserve separate memory segments for each member when they are created, a union reserves a single memory space for its largest member, thereby providing a memory-saving feature for members to share the same memory space.

Unions are created with the keyword union and contain member definitions similar to that of structures. The next block of program code creates a union definition for a phone book.

```
union phoneBook {

    char *name;
    char *number;
    char *address;

};
```

Like structures, union members are accessed via the dot operator, as the next program demonstrates.

```
#include <stdio.h>

union phoneBook {
```

```
    char *name;
    char *number;
    char *address;

};

struct magazine {

    char *name;
    char *author;
    int isbn;

};

main()

{

    union phoneBook aBook;
    struct magazine aMagazine;

    printf("\nUnion Details\n");
    printf("Address for aBook.name: %p\n", &aBook.name);
    printf("Address for aBook.number: %p\n", &aBook.number);
    printf("Address for aBook.address: %p\n", &aBook.address);

    printf("\nStructure Details\n");
    printf("Address for aMagazine.name: %p\n", &aMagazine.name);
    printf("Address for aMagazine.author: %p\n", &aMagazine.author);
    printf("Address for aMagazine.isbn: %p\n", &aMagazine.isbn);

} //end main
```

The output of the preceding program is shown in Figure 9.6, which reveals how memory allocation is conducted between unions and structures. Each member of the union shares the same memory space.

```
C:\
Administrator@MUINE ~
$ ./a

Union Details
Address for aBook.name: 0x22ccdc
Address for aBook.number: 0x22ccdc
Address for aBook.address: 0x22ccdc

Structure Details
Address for aMagazine.name: 0x22ccc0
Address for aMagazine.author: 0x22ccc4
Address for aMagazine.isbn: 0x22ccc8

Administrator@MUINE ~
$ ■
```

FIGURE 9.6

Comparing memory allocation between structures and unions.

TYPE CASTING

Although it is not supported by all high-level programming languages, type casting is a powerful feature of C. *Type casting* enables C programmers to force one variable of a certain type to be another type, an important consideration especially when dealing with integer division. For all its power, type casting is simple to use. As demonstrated next, just surround a data-type name with parentheses followed by the data or variable for which you want to type cast.

```
int x = 12;
int y = 5;
float result = 0;

result = (float) x / (float) y;
```

 TIP   Hollywood does a lot of type casting!

The next program and its output (shown in Figure 9.7) further demonstrate the use of type casting, and in addition show what happens when type casting is not leveraged during integer division.

```
#include <stdio.h>

main()

{

    int x = 12;
    int y = 5;
```

```
    printf("\nWithout Type-Casting\n");
    printf("12 \\ 5 = %.2f\n", x/y);

    printf("\nWith Type-Casting\n");
    printf("12 \\ 5 = %.2f\n", (float) x / (float) y);

} //end main
```

TIP Remember that the backslash (\) is a reserved and special character in the printf() function. To incorporate a backslash character in your output, use the \\ conversion specifier shown next.

```
printf("12 \\ 5 = %.2f\n", (float) x / (float) y);
```

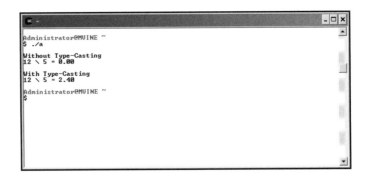

FIGURE 9.7

Conducting integer division with and without type casting.

As you might expect, type casting is not limited to numbers. You can also type cast numbers to characters and characters to numbers, as shown next.

```
#include <stdio.h>

main()

{

    int number = 86;
    char letter = 'M';

    printf("\n86 type-casted to char is: %c\n", (char) number);
```

```
    printf("\n'M' type-casted to int is: %d\n ", (int) letter);

} //end main
```

Figure 9.8 demonstrates the output from the preceding program in which a number is type casted to a character and a character is type casted to a number.

 TIP C always prints the ASCII equivalent of a letter when using the %n conversion specifier with a character equivalent. In addition, C always prints the character equivalent of an ASCII number when using the %c conversion specifier with an ASCII equivalent.

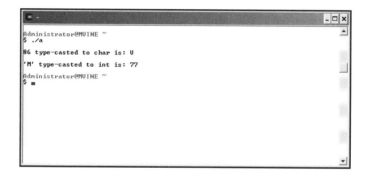

FIGURE 9.8

Type casting numbers to characters and characters to numbers.

CHAPTER PROGRAM—CARD SHUFFLE

The Card Shuffle program uses many chapter-based concepts, such as structures, arrays of structures, and passing structures to functions, to build an easy card-shuffling program. Specifically, the Card Shuffle program initializes 52 poker cards using an array of structures. It then uses various techniques, such as random numbers and user-defined functions, to build a shuffle routine, which after shuffling deals five random cards.

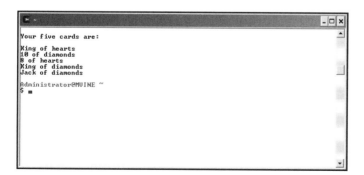

FIGURE 9.9

Using chapter-based concepts to build the Card Shuffle program.

After studying the Card Shuffle program you should be able to use it in your own card games to shuffle and deal cards for Poker games and others, such as Five Card Draw, Black Jack.

All of the code required to build the Card Shuffle program is shown next.

```c
#include <stdio.h>
#include <time.h>
#include <string.h>

//define new data type
typedef struct deck {

    char type[10];
    char used;
    int value;

} aDeck; //end type

//function prototype
void shuffle( aDeck * );

main()

{

    int x,y;

    aDeck myDeck[52];

    srand( time( NULL ) );

    //initialize structure array
    for ( x = 0; x < 3; x++ ) {

        for ( y = 0; y < 13; y++ ) {

            switch (x) {

                case 0:
                    strcpy(myDeck[y].type, "diamonds");
```

```
            myDeck[y].value = y;
            myDeck[y].used = 'n';
            break;

        case 1:

            strcpy(myDeck[y + 13].type, "clubs");
            myDeck[y + 13].value = y;
            myDeck[y + 13].used = 'n';
            break;

        case 2:
            strcpy(myDeck[y + 26].type, "hearts");
            myDeck[y + 26].value = y;
            myDeck[y + 26].used = 'n';
            break;

        case 3:
            strcpy(myDeck[y + 39].type, "spades");
            myDeck[y + 39].value = y;
            myDeck[y + 39].used = 'n';
            break;

        } //end switch

    } // end inner loop

  } // end outer loop

  shuffle( myDeck );

} //end main

void shuffle( aDeck * thisDeck )

{

    int x;
```

```c
int iRnd;
int found = 0;

system("clear");
printf("\nYour five cards are: \n\n");

while ( found < 5 ) {

   iRnd = rand() % 51;

  if ( thisDeck[iRnd].used == 'n' ) {

      switch (thisDeck[iRnd].value) {

        case 12:
           printf("Ace of %s\n", thisDeck[iRnd].type);
           break;

        case 11:
           printf("King of %s\n", thisDeck[iRnd].type);
           break;

        case 10:
           printf("Queen of %s\n", thisDeck[iRnd].type);
           break;

        case 9:
           printf("Jack of %s\n", thisDeck[iRnd].type);
           break;

         default:
            printf("%d of ", thisDeck[iRnd].value + 2);
            printf("%s\n", thisDeck[iRnd].type);
            break;

      }  // end switch

   thisDeck[iRnd].used = 'y';
```

```
    found = found + 1;

    } //end if

  }  // end while loop

} //end shuffle
```

Summary

- Structures are a collection of variables related in nature, but not necessarily in data type.
- Structures are most commonly used to define an object—a person, a place, a thing—or similarly a record in a database or file.
- The first process in creating a structure is to build the structure definition using the `struct` keyword followed by braces, with individual variables defined as members.
- Members of structures are the individual elements or variables that make up a collection of variables.
- Structure tags identify the structure and can be used to create instances of the structure.
- When structure definitions are created using the `struct` keyword, memory is not allocated for the structure until an instance of the structure is created.
- The `typedef` keyword is used for creating structure definitions to build an alias relationship with the structure tag (structure name). It provides a shortcut for programmers when creating instances of the structure.
- To create an array of structures, supply the desired number of array elements surrounded by brackets after the structure definition.
- Structures can be passed to functions via pass by value for read-only access and pass by reference for modifying structure member contents.
- Passing by value protects an incoming variable's value by sending a copy of the original data rather than the actual variable to the function.
- Passing by reference sends a variable's memory address to a function, which allows statements in the function to modify the original variable's memory contents.
- The structure pointer operator is a dash followed by the greater-than sign with no space in between (`->`).
- The structure pointer operator is used to access a structure member through a pointer.
- Passing arrays of structures to functions is automatically passing by reference; it is also known as passing by address. This is true because an array name is a pointer.

- Unions provide a more economical way to build objects with attributes by reserving a single memory space for its largest member.
- Type casting enables C programmers to force one variable of a certain type to be another type.

CHALLENGES

1. Create a structure called car with the following members:

   - make
   - model
   - year
   - miles

   Create an instance of the car structure named myCar and assign data to each of the members. Print the contents of each member to standard output using the printf() function.

2. Using the car structure from challenge number one, create a structure array with three elements named myCars. Populate each structure in the array with your favorite car model information. Use a for loop to print each structure detail in the array.

3. Create a program that uses a structure array to hold contact information for your friends. The program should allow the user to enter up to five friends and print the phone book's current entries. Create functions to add entries in the phone book and to print valid phone book entries. Do not display phone book entries that are invalid or NULL (0).

DYNAMIC MEMORY ALLOCATION

I n this chapter I will show you how C uses system resources to allocate, reallocate, and free memory. You will learn basic memory concepts and also how C library functions and operators can take advantage of system resources, such as RAM and virtual memory.

Specifically, this chapter covers the following topics:

- Memory concepts continued
- `sizeof`
- `malloc()`
- `calloc()`
- `realloc()`

MEMORY CONCEPTS CONTINUED

This chapter is dedicated to discussing dynamic memory concepts, such as allocating, reallocating, and freeing memory using the functions `malloc()`, `calloc()`, `realloc()`, and `free()`. This section specifically reviews essential memory concepts that directly relate to how these functions receive and use memory.

Software programs, including operating systems, use a variety of memory implementations, including virtual memory and RAM. Random access memory (RAM) provides a volatile solution for allocating, storing, and retrieving data. RAM is considered volatile because of its inability to store data after the computer loses power (shuts down). Another volatile memory storage area is called virtual memory. Essentially, virtual memory is a reserved section of your hard disk in which the operating system can swap memory segments. Virtual memory is not as efficient as random access memory, but it provides an impression to the CPU that it has more memory than it really does. Increasing memory resources through virtual memory provides the operating system an inexpensive solution for dynamic memory demands.

 TIP *Virtual memory* increases the perception of more memory by using hard-disk space for swapping memory segments.

Stack and Heap

Using a combination of RAM and virtual memory, all software programs use their own area of memory called the *stack*. Every time a function is called in a program, the function's variables and parameters are pushed onto the program's memory stack and then pushed off or "popped" when the function has completed or returned.

 TIP Used for storing variable and parameter contents, *memory stacks* are dynamic groupings of memory that grow and shrink as each program allocates and de-allocates memory.

After software programs have terminated, memory is returned for reuse for other software and system programs. Moreover, the operating system is responsible for managing this realm of unallocated memory, known as the *heap*. Software programs that can leverage memory-allocating functions like `malloc()`, `calloc()`, and `realloc()` use the heap.

 TIP The *heap* is an area of unused memory managed by the operating system.

Once a program frees memory, it is returned back to the heap for further use by the same program or other programs.

In a nutshell, memory allocating functions and the heap are extremely important to C programmers because they allow you to control a program's memory consumption and allocation. The remainder of this chapter will show you how to retrieve and return memory to and from the heap.

SIZEOF

There will be occasions when you need to know how large a variable or data type is. This is especially important in C, because C allows programmers to create memory resources dynamically. More specifically, it is imperative for C programmers to know how many bytes a system uses to store data, such as integers, floats, or doubles, because not all systems use the same amount of space for storing data. The C standard library provides the sizeof operator to assist programmers in this type of situation. When used in your programs, the sizeof operator will help you build a more system-independent software program.

The sizeof operator takes a variable name or data type as an argument and returns the number of bytes required to store the data in memory. The next program, and its output shown in Figure 10.1, demonstrates a simple use of the sizeof operator.

```c
#include <stdio.h>

main()

{

    int x;
    float f;
    double d;
    char c;

    typedef struct employee {

        int id;
        char *name;
        float salary;

    } e;

    printf("\nSize of integer: %d bytes\n", sizeof(x));
    printf("Size of float: %d bytes\n", sizeof(f));
    printf("Size of double %d bytes\n", sizeof(d));
    printf("Size of char %d byte\n", sizeof(c));
    printf("Size of employee structure: %d bytes\n", sizeof(e));

} //end main
```

FIGURE 10.1

Using the sizeof operator to determine storage requirements.

The sizeof operator can take either a variable name or a data type, as shown next.

```
int x;
printf("\nSize of integer: %d bytes\n", sizeof(x)); //valid variable name
printf("\nSize of integer: %d bytes\n", sizeof(int)); //valid data type
```

The sizeof operator can also be used to determine the memory requirements of arrays. Using simple arithmetic, you can determine how many elements are contained in an array by dividing the array size by the size of the array data type, as demonstrated in the next program and its output in Figure 10.2.

```
#include <stdio.h>

main()

{

    int array[10];

    printf("\nSize of array: %d bytes\n", sizeof(array));
    printf("Number of elements in array ");
    printf("%d\n", sizeof(array) / sizeof(int));

} //end main
```

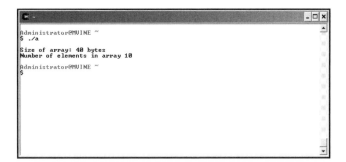

MALLOC()

Sometimes it is impossible to know exactly how much memory your program will need for a given function. Fixed-sized arrays may not be large enough to hold the amount of data you are requesting to store. For example, what would happen if you created an eight-element, fixed-size character array to hold a user's name, and the user enters the name "Alexandria"— a 10-character name with an 11th character required for null. Best-case scenario: You incorporated error checking in your program to prevent a user from entering a string larger than eight characters. Worst-case scenario: The user's information is sent elsewhere in memory, potentially overwriting other data.

There are many reasons for dynamically creating and using memory, such as creating and reading strings from standard input, dynamic arrays, and other dynamic data structures such as linked lists. C provides a few functions for creating dynamic memory, one of which is the malloc() function. The malloc() function is part of the standard library <stdlib.h> and takes a number as an argument. When executed, malloc() attempts to retrieve designated memory segments from the heap and returns a pointer that is the starting point for the memory reserved. Basic malloc() use is demonstrated in the next program.

```
#include <stdio.h>
#include <stdlib.h>

main()

{

    char *name;

    name = malloc(80);

} //end main
```

The preceding program's use of malloc() is not quite complete because some C compilers may require that you perform type casting when assigning dynamic memory to a variable. To eliminate potential compiler warnings, I will modify the previous program to simply use a pointer of type char in a type cast, as demonstrated next.

```c
#include <stdio.h>
#include <stdlib.h>

main()

{

    char *name;

    name = (char *) malloc(80);

} //end main
```

 HINT The malloc() function returns a null pointer if it is unsuccessful in allocating memory.

Better yet, we should be more specific when creating dynamic memory by explicitly telling the system the size of the data type for which we are requesting memory. In other words, we should incorporate the sizeof operator in our dynamic memory allocation, as shown next.

```c
#include <stdio.h>
#include <stdlib.h>

main()

{

    char *name;

    name = (char *) malloc(80 * sizeof(char));

} //end main
```

Using the sizeof operator explicitly tells the system that you want 80 bytes of type char, which happens to be a 1-byte data type on most systems.

You should also always check that malloc() was successful before attempting to use the memory. To test the malloc() function's outcome, simply use an if condition to test for a NULL pointer, as revealed next.

```c
#include <stdio.h>
#include <stdlib.h>

main()

{

   char *name;

   name = (char *) malloc(80 * sizeof(char));

   if ( name == NULL )
      printf("\nOut of memory!\n");
   else
      printf("\nMemory allocated.\n");

} //end main
```

After studying the preceding program, you can see that the keyword NULL is used to compare the pointer. If the pointer is NULL, the malloc() function was not successful in allocating memory.

 CAUTION Always check for valid results when attempting to allocate memory. Failure to test the pointer returned by memory allocating functions such as malloc() can result in abnormal software or system behavior.

Managing Strings with malloc()

As mentioned in Chapter 8, "Strings," dynamic memory allocation allows programmers to create and use strings when reading information from standard input. To do so, simply use the malloc() function and assign its result to a pointer of char type prior to reading information from the keyboard.

Using malloc() to create and read strings from standard input is demonstrated in the next program (see Figure 10.3).

```c
#include <stdio.h>
#include <stdlib.h>

main()

{

    char *name;

    name = (char *) malloc(80*sizeof(char));

    if ( name != NULL ) {

        printf("\nEnter your name: ");
        gets(name);

        printf("\nHi %s\n", name);

    }  // end if

} //end main
```

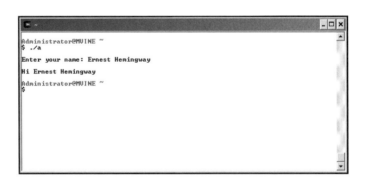

FIGURE 10.3

Using dynamic memory to read character strings from standard input.

This program allows a user to enter up to an 80-character name, the amount of storage requested by the `malloc()` function, for the character string.

Freeing Memory

Good programming practice dictates that you free memory after using it. For this reason, the C standard library offers the `free()` function, which takes a pointer as an argument and frees the memory the pointer refers to. This allows your system to reuse the memory for other software applications or other `malloc()` function calls, as demonstrated next.

```c
#include <stdio.h>
#include <stdlib.h>

main()

{

    char *name;

    name = (char *) malloc(80*sizeof(char));

    if ( name != NULL ) {

        printf("\nEnter your name: ");
        gets(name);

        printf("\nHi %s\n", name);

        free(name); //free memory resources

    }  // end if

} //end main
```

Freeing memory allocated by functions such as `malloc()` is an important housekeeping duty of C programmers. Even with today's memory-rich systems it's a good idea to free memory as soon as you no longer need it because the more memory you consume the less that is available for other processes. If you forget to release allocated or used memory in your programs, most operating systems will clean up for you. This benefit, however, only applies after your program terminates. It is the programmer's responsibility, however, to free memory once it is no longer needed. Failure to release memory in your programs can result in unnecessary or wasted memory that is not returned to the heap, also known as a memory leak.

TIP   Memory allocated by malloc() will continue to exist until program termination or until a programmer "frees" it with the free() function. To release a block of memory with the free() function the memory must have been previously allocated (returned) by malloc() or calloc().

Working with Memory Segments

Individual memory segments acquired by malloc() can be treated much like array members; these memory segments can be referenced with indexes, as demonstrated in the next program and its output shown in Figure 10.4.

```c
#include <stdio.h>
#include <stdlib.h>

main()

{

    int *numbers;
    int x;

    numbers = (int *) malloc(5 * sizeof(int));

    if ( numbers == NULL )
        return;   // return if malloc is not successful

    numbers[0] = 100;
    numbers[1] = 200;
    numbers[2] = 300;
    numbers[3] = 400;
    numbers[4] = 500;

    printf("\nIndividual memory segments initialized to:\n");

    for ( x = 0; x < 5; x++ )
        printf("numbers[%d] = %d\n", x, numbers[x]);

} //end main
```

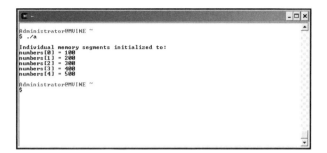

FIGURE 10.4

Using indexes and array concepts to work with memory segments.

Simply supply the pointer name with an index to initialize and access segments of memory. To reiterate, memory segments can be accessed via indexes similar to array elements. This is a useful and powerful concept for dissecting chunks of memory.

CALLOC() AND REALLOC()

Another memory allocating tool is the C standard library `<stdlib.h>` function `calloc()`. Like the `malloc()` function, the `calloc()` function attempts to grab contiguous segments of memory from the heap. The `calloc()` function takes two arguments: the first determines the number of memory segments needed and the second is the size of the data type.

A basic implementation of the `calloc()` function is established in the next program.

```
#include <stdio.h>
#include <stdlib.h>

main()

{

   int *numbers;


   numbers = (int *) calloc(10, sizeof(int));

   if ( numbers == NULL )
      return;  // return if calloc is not successful

} //end main
```

I can use the `calloc()` function to obtain a chunk of memory to hold 10 integer data types by passing two arguments. The first argument tells `calloc()` I want 10 contiguous memory segments and the second argument tells C that the data types need to be the size of an integer data type on the machine it's running.

The main benefit of using calloc() rather than malloc() is calloc()'s ability to initialize each memory segment allocated. This is an important feature because malloc() requires that the programmer be responsible for initializing memory before using it.

At first glance, both malloc() and calloc() appear to be dynamic in memory allocation, and they are to some degree, yet they fall somewhat short in their ability to expand memory originally allocated. For example, say you allocated five integer memory segments and filled them with data. Later, the program requires that you add five more memory segments to the original block allocated by malloc() while preserving the original contents. This is an interesting dilemma. You could, of course, allocate more memory using a separate pointer, but that would not allow you to treat both memory blocks as a contiguous memory area and, therefore, would prevent you from accessing all memory segments as a single array. Fortunately, the realloc() function provides a way to expand contiguous blocks of memory while preserving the original contents.

As shown next, the realloc() function takes two arguments for parameters and returns a pointer as output.

```
newPointer = realloc(oldPointer, 10 * sizeof(int));
```

realloc()'s first argument takes the original pointer set by malloc() or calloc(). The second argument describes the total amount of memory you want to allocate.

Like the malloc() and calloc() functions, realloc() is an easy-to-use function, but it does require some spot-checking after it executes. Specifically, there are three scenarios for realloc()'s outcome, which Table 10.1 describes.

TABLE 10.1   POSSIBLE REALLOC() OUTCOMES

Scenario	Outcome
Successful without move	Same pointer returned
Successful with move	New pointer returned
Not successful	NULL pointer returned

If realloc() is successful in expanding the contiguous memory, it returns the original pointer set by malloc() or calloc(). There will be times, however, when realloc() is unable to expand the original contiguous memory and will, therefore, seek another area in memory where it can allocate the number of contiguous memory segments for both the previous data and the new memory requested. When this happens, realloc() copies the original memory contents into the new contiguous memory locations and returns a new pointer to the new starting location. Be aware that there will be times when realloc() is not successful in any of its attempts to expand contiguous memory and ultimately will return a NULL pointer.

Your best bet for testing the outcome of realloc() is testing for NULL. If a NULL pointer is not returned, you can assign the pointer back to the old pointer, which then contains the starting address of the expanded contiguous memory.

The concept of expanding contiguous memory and testing realloc()'s outcome is demonstrated in the next program, with the output shown in Figure 10.5.

```c
#include<stdio.h>
#include<stdlib.h>

main()

{

    int *number;
    int *newNumber;
    int x;

    number = malloc(sizeof(int) * 5);

    if ( number == NULL ) {

        printf("\nOut of memory!\n");
        return;

    }  // end if

    printf("\nOriginal memory:\n");
    for ( x = 0; x < 5; x++ ) {

        number[x] = x * 100;
        printf("number[%d] = %d\n", x, number[x]);
```

```
}   // end for loop

newNumber = realloc(number, 10 * sizeof(int));

if ( newNumber == NULL ) {

   printf("\nOut of memory!\n");
   return;

}

else

   number = newNumber;

//intialize new memory only
for ( x = 5; x < 10; x++ )
   number[x] = x * 100;

printf("\nExpanded memory:\n");
for ( x = 0; x < 10; x++ )
   printf("number[%d] = %d\n", x, number[x]);

//free memory
free(number);

}   // end main
```

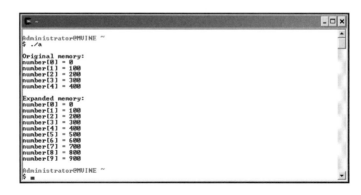

FIGURE 10.5

Using realloc() to expand contiguous memory segments.

After studying the preceding program and Figure 10.5, you can see that realloc() is quite useful for expanding contiguous memory while preserving original memory contents.

CHAPTER PROGRAM—MATH QUIZ

Shown in Figure 10.6, the Math Quiz game uses memory allocation techniques, such as the calloc() and free() functions, to build a fun and dynamic quiz that tests the player's ability to answer basic addition problems. After studying the Math Quiz program, you can use your own dynamic memory allocation and random number techniques to build fun quiz programs of any nature.

FIGURE 10.6

Using chapter-based concepts to build the Math Quiz.

All of the code required to build the Math Quiz game is demonstrated next.

```c
#include <stdio.h>
#include <stdlib.h>
#include <time.h>

main()

{

    int response;
    int *answer;
    int *op1;
    int *op2;
    char *result;
    int x;
```

```
srand(time(NULL));

printf("\nMath Quiz\n\n");
printf("Enter # of problems: ");
scanf("%d", &response);

/* Based on the number of questions the user wishes to take,
    allocate enough memory to hold question data. */

op1 = (int *) calloc(response, sizeof(int));
op2 = (int *) calloc(response, sizeof(int));
answer = (int *) calloc(response, sizeof(int));
result = (char *) calloc(response, sizeof(char));

if ( op1 == NULL || op2 == NULL || answer == NULL || result == NULL ) {

    printf("\nOut of Memory!\n");
    return;

}  // end if

//display random addition problems

for ( x = 0; x < response; x++ ) {

    op1[x] = rand() % 100;
    op2[x] = rand() % 100;

    printf("\n%d + %d = ", op1[x], op2[x]);

    scanf("%d", &answer[x]);

    if ( answer[x] == op1[x] + op2[x] )

        result[x] = 'c';

    else
```

```
        result[x] = 'i';

    } // end for loop

  printf("\nQuiz Results\n");
  printf("\nQuestion\tYour Answer\tCorrect\n");

  //print the results of the quiz

  for ( x = 0; x < response; x++ ) {

     if ( result[x] == 'c' )

        printf("%d + %d\t\t%d\t\tYes\n", op1[x], op2[x], answer[x]);

     else

        printf("%d + %d\t\t%d\t\tNo\n", op1[x], op2[x], answer[x]);

  }  //end for loop

  //free memory
  free(op1);
  free(op2);
  free(answer);
  free(result);

} // end main
```

Summary

- Random access memory (RAM) provides a volatile solution for allocating, storing, and retrieving data. RAM is considered volatile because of its inability to store data after the computer loses power (shuts down).
- Another volatile memory storage area called virtual memory is a reserved section of the hard disk in which the operating system can swap memory segments.
- Virtual memory is not as efficient as random access memory, but it does provide an impression to the CPU that is has more memory that it really does.

- Used for storing variable and parameter contents, memory stacks are dynamic groupings of memory that grow and shrink as each program allocates and de-allocates memory.
- The heap is an area of unused memory managed by the operating system.
- The sizeof operator takes a variable name or data type as an argument and returns the number of bytes required to store the data in memory.
- The sizeof operator can also be used to determine the memory requirements of arrays.
- The malloc() function attempts to retrieve designated memory segments from the heap and returns a pointer that is the starting point for the memory reserved.
- The malloc() function returns a null pointer if it is unsuccessful in allocating memory.
- Individual memory segments acquired by malloc() can be treated much like array members; these memory segments can be referenced with indexes.
- The free() function takes a pointer as an argument and frees the memory the pointer refers to.
- Like the malloc() function, the calloc() function attempts to grab contiguous segments of memory from the heap. The calloc() function takes two arguments: the first determines the number of memory segments needed and the second is the size of the data type.
- The main benefit of using calloc() rather than malloc() is calloc()'s ability to initialize each memory segment allocated.
- The realloc() function provides a feature for expanding contiguous blocks of memory while preserving the original contents.

CHALLENGES

1. Create a program that uses `malloc()` to allocate a chunk of memory to hold a string no larger than 80 characters. Prompt the user to enter his favorite movie. Read his response with `scanf()` and assign the data to your newly allocated memory. Display the user's favorite movie back to standard output.

2. Using the `calloc()` function, write a program that reads a user's name from standard input. Use a loop to iterate through the memory allocated counting the number of characters in the user's name. The loop should stop when a memory segment is reached that was not used in reading and storing the user's name. (Remember, `calloc()` initializes all memory allocated.) Print to standard output the number of characters in the user's name.

3. Create a phone book program that allows users to enter names and phone numbers of friends and acquaintances. Create a structure to hold contact information and use `calloc()` to reserve the first memory segment. The user should be able to add or modify phone book entries through a menu. Use the `realloc()` function to add contiguous memory segments to the original memory block when a user adds a new phone book entry.

FILE INPUT AND OUTPUT

I n this chapter, I will show you how to open, read, and write information to data files using functions from the standard input/output (<stdio.h>) library. You will also learn essential data file hierarchy concepts and how C uses file streams to manage data files.

Specifically, this chapter covers the following topics:

- Introduction to data files
- File streams
- goto and error handling

INTRODUCTION TO DATA FILES

Assuming you've been reading the chapters of this book in order, you've already learned the basics of utilizing C and volatile memory storage devices for saving, retrieving, and editing data. Specifically, you know that variables are used to manage data in volatile memory areas, such as random access memory and virtual memory, and that memory can be dynamically obtained for temporarily storing data.

Despite the obvious importance of volatile memory such as RAM, it does have its drawbacks when it comes to long-term data storage. When data needs to be archived or stored in nonvolatile memory areas such as a hard disk, programmers look to data files as a viable answer for storing and retrieving data after the computer's power has been turned off.

Data files are often text-based and are used for storing and retrieving related information like that stored in a database. Managing the information contained in data files is up to the C programmer. In order to understand how files can be managed, I will introduce you to beginning concepts that are used to build files and record layouts for basic data file management.

It's important to understand the breakdown and hierarchy of data files, because each component (parent) and sub component (child) are used together to create the whole. Without each component and its hierarchical relationships, building more advanced data file systems such as relational databases would be difficult.

A common data file hierarchy is typically broken down into five categories as described in Table 11.1.

TABLE 11.1 DATA FILE HIERARCHY	
Entity	**Description**
Bit	Binary digit, 0 or 1
Byte	Eight characters
Field	Grouping of bytes
Record	Grouping of fields
File	Grouping of records

Bits and Bytes

Also known as binary digits, *bits* are the smallest value in a data file. Each bit value can only be a 0 or 1. Because bits are the smallest unit of measurement in computer systems, they provide an easy mechanism for electrical circuits to duplicate 1s and 0s with patterns of *off* and *on* electrical states. When grouped together, bits can build the next unit of data management, known as bytes.

Bytes provide the next step in the data file food chain. Bytes are made up of eight bits and are used to store a single character, such as a number, a letter, or any other character found in a character set. For example, a single byte might contain the letter M, the number 7, or a keyboard character such as the exclamation point (!). Together, bytes make up words or, better yet, fields.

Fields, Records, and Files

In database or data-file lingo, groupings of characters are most commonly referred to as *fields*. Fields are often recognized as placeholders on a graphical user interface (GUI), but are really a data concept that groups characters in a range of sizes and data types to provide meaningful information. Fields could be a person's name, social security number, street address, phone number, and so on. For example, the name "Sheila" could be a value stored in a field called First Name. When combined in a logical group, fields can be used to express a record of information.

Records are logical groupings of fields that comprise a single row of information. Each field in a record describes the record's attributes. For example, a student record might be comprised of name, age, ID, major, and GPA fields. Each field is unique in description but together describes a single record.

Individual fields in records are sometimes separated or delimited using spaces, tabs, or commas as shown in the next sample record that lists field values for a single student.

```
Sheila Vine, 29, 555-55-5555, Computer Science, 4.0
```

Together, records are stored in data files.

Data files are comprised of one or more records and are at the top of the data file food chain. Each record in a file typically describes a unique collection of fields. Files can be used to store all types of information, such as student or employee data. Data files are normally associated with various database processes in which information can be managed in nonvolatile states, such as a local disk drive, USB flash device, or web server. An example data file called `students.dat` with comma-delimited records is shown next.

```
Michael Vine, 30, 222-22-2222, Political Science, 3.5
Sheila Vine, 29, 555-55-5555, Computer Science, 4.0
Spencer Vine, 19, 777-77-7777, Law, 3.8
Olivia Vine, 18, 888-88-8888, Medicine, 4.0
```

FILE STREAMS

Pointers, pointers, and more pointers! You know you love them, or at least by now love to hate them. As you may have guessed, anything worth doing in C involves pointers. And of course data files are no exception.

C programmers use pointers to manage streams that read and write data. Understanding streams is quite easy. In fact, *streams* are just file or hardware devices, such as a monitor or printer, which can be controlled by C programmers using pointers to the stream.

To point to and manage a file stream in C, simply use an internal data structure called FILE. Pointers of type FILE are created just like any other variable, as the next program demonstrates.

```c
#include <stdio.h>

main()

{

    //create 3 file pointers
    FILE *pRead;
    FILE *pWrite;
    FILE *pAppend;

} //end main
```

As you can see, I created three FILE pointer variables called pRead, pWrite, and pAppend. Using a series of functions that I will show you soon, each FILE pointer can open and manage a separate data file.

Opening and Closing Files

The basic components for file processing involve opening, processing, and closing data files. Opening a data file should always involve a bit of error checking and/or handling. Failure to test the results of a file-open attempt will sometimes cause unwanted program results in your software.

To open a data file, use the standard input/output library function fopen(). The fopen() function is used in an assignment statement to pass a FILE pointer to a previously declared FILE pointer, as the next program reveals.

```c
#include <stdio.h>

main()

{

    FILE *pRead;
```

```
    pRead = fopen("file1.dat", "r");

} //end main
```

This program uses the `fopen()` function to open a data file, called `file1.dat`, in a read-only manner (more on this in a moment). The `fopen()` function returns a `FILE` pointer back to the `pRead` variable.

DATA FILE EXTENSIONS

It is common to name data files with a `.dat` extension, although it is not required. Many data files used for processing information have other extensions, such as `.txt` for text files, `.csv` for comma separated value files, `.ini` for initialization files, or `.log` for log files.

You can create your own data file programs that use file extensions of your choice. For example, I could write my own personal finance software program that opens, reads, and writes to a data file called `finance.mpf`, in which `.mpf` stands for Michael's personal finance.

As demonstrated in the previous program, the `fopen()` function takes two arguments: the first supplies `fopen()` with the file name to open, and the second argument tells `fopen()` how to open the file.

Table 11.2 depicts a few common options for opening text files using `fopen()`.

TABLE 11.2   COMMON TEXT FILE OPEN MODES

Mode	Description
r	Opens file for reading
w	Creates file for writing; discards any previous data
a	Writes to end of file (append)

After opening a file, you should always check to ensure that the `FILE` pointer was returned successfully. In other words, you want to check for occasions when the specified file name cannot be found. Does the Window's error "Disk not ready or File not found" sound familiar? To test `fopen()`'s return value, test for a `NULL` value in a condition, as demonstrated next.

```
#include <stdio.h>

main()

{

   FILE *pRead;

   pRead = fopen("file1.dat", "r");

   if ( pRead == NULL )

      printf("\nFile cannot be opened\n");

   else

      printf("\nFile opened for reading\n");

} //end main
```

TIP

The following condition

```
if ( pRead == NULL )
```

can be shortened with the next condition.

```
if ( pRead )
```

If pRead returns a non-NULL, the if condition is true. If pRead returns NULL, the condition is false.

After successfully opening and processing a file, you should close the file using a function called fclose(). The fclose() function uses the FILE pointer to flush the stream and close the file. As shown next, the fclose() function takes a FILE pointer name as an argument.

```
fclose(pRead);
```

In sections to come, I will show you more of the fopen() and fclose() functions and how they can be used for managing the reading, writing, and appending of information in data files.

Reading Data

You can easily create your own data files using common text editors such as vi, nano, or even Microsoft's Notepad. If you're using a Microsoft Windows operating system, you can also use a Microsoft DOS-based system function called copy con, which copies text entered via the keyboard into a predetermined file. The copy con process copies text entered from the console and appends an end-of-file marker using Ctrl+Z, as demonstrated in Figure 11.1.

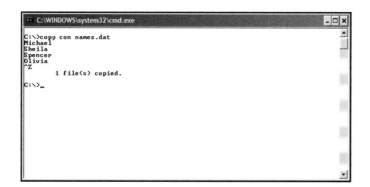

FIGURE 11.1

Using Microsoft's copy con process to create a data file.

To read a data file, you will need to investigate a few new functions. Specifically, I will show you how to read a file's contents and check for the file's EOF (end-of-file) marker using the functions fscanf() and feof().

To demonstrate, study the following program that reads a data file called names.dat until an end-of-file marker is read. The output is shown in Figure 11.2.

```c
#include <stdio.h>

main()

{

    FILE *pRead;
    char name[10];

    pRead = fopen("names.dat", "r");

    if ( pRead == NULL )

        printf("\nFile cannot be opened\n");
```

```
else

    printf("\nContents of names.dat\n\n");
    fscanf(pRead, "%s", name);

    while ( !feof(pRead) ) {

        printf("%s\n", name);
        fscanf(pRead, "%s", name);

    }   //end loop

} //end main
```

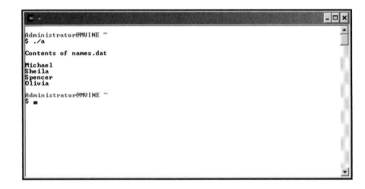

FIGURE 11.2

Reading
information from
a data file.

After successfully opening names.dat, I use the fscanf() function to read a single field within
the file. The fscanf() function is similar to the scanf() function but works with FILE streams
and takes three arguments: a FILE pointer, a data type, and a variable to store the retrieved
value in. After reading the record, I can use the printf() function to display data from the file.

Most data files contain more than one record. To read multiple records, it is common to use
a looping structure that can read all records until a condition is met. If you want to read all
records until the end-of-file is met, the feof() function provides a nice solution. Using the
not operator (!), you can pass the FILE pointer to the feof() function and loop until the function returns a non-zero value when an end-of-file marker is reached.

fscanf() can also read records containing multiple fields by supplying to the second argument a series of type specifiers for each field in the record. For example, the next fscanf()
function expects to read two character strings called name and hobby.

```
fscanf(pRead, "%s%s", name, hobby);
```

The %s type specifier will read a series of characters until a white space is found, including blank, new line, or tab.

Other valid type specifiers you can use with the fscanf() function are listed in Table 11.3.

TABLE 11.3 FSCANF() TYPE SPECIFIERS

Type	Description
c	Single character
d	Decimal integer
e, E, f, g, G	Floating point
o	Octal integer
s	String of characters
u	Unsigned decimal integer
x, X	Hexadecimal integer

To demonstrate how a file containing records with multiple fields is read, study the next program and its output in Figure 11.3.

```c
#include <stdio.h>

main()

{

    FILE *pRead;
    char name[10];
    char hobby[15];

    pRead = fopen("hobbies.dat", "r");

    if ( pRead == NULL )

        printf("\nFile cannot be opened\n");

    else
```

```
    printf("\nName\tHobby\n\n");
    fscanf(pRead, "%s%s", name, hobby);

    while ( !feof(pRead) ) {

        printf("%s\t%s\n", name, hobby);
        fscanf(pRead, "%s%s", name, hobby);

    }  //end loop

} //end main
```

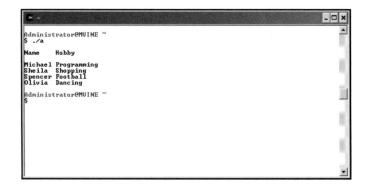

FIGURE 11.3

Reading records in a data file with multiple fields.

Writing Data

Writing information to a data file is just as easy as reading data. In fact, you can use a function similar to printf() called fprintf() that uses a FILE pointer to write data to a file. The fprintf() function takes a FILE pointer, a list of data types, and a list of values (or variables) to write information to a data file, as demonstrated in the next program and in Figure 11.4.

```
#include <stdio.h>

main()

{

    FILE *pWrite;

    char fName[20];
    char lName[20];
```

```
    char id[15];
    float gpa;

    pWrite = fopen("students.dat", "w");

    if ( pWrite == NULL )

        printf("\nFile not opened\n");

    else {

        printf("\nEnter first name, last name, id and GPA\n\n");
        printf("Enter data separated by spaces: ");

        //store data entered by the user into variables
        scanf("%s%s%s%f", fName, lName, id, &gpa);

        //write variable contents separated by tabs
        fprintf(pWrite, "%s\t%s\t%s\t%.2f\n", fName, lName, id, gpa);

        fclose(pWrite);

    }   //end if

}  //end main
```

FIGURE 11.4

Writing a record of information to a data file.

In the preceding program I ask the user to enter student information. Each piece of information is considered a field in the record and is separated during input with a single space character. In other words, I am able to read an entire line of data using a single scanf() function with the user entering multiple pieces of data separated by spaces. After reading each field of data, I use the fprintf() function to write variables to a data file called students.dat. By separating each field in the record with a tab (I've created a tab-delimited file), I can easily read the same record back with the following program.

```c
#include <stdio.h>

main()

{

    FILE *pRead;

    char fName[20];
    char lName[20];
    char id[15];
    float gpa;

    pRead = fopen("students.dat", "r");

    if ( pRead == NULL )

        printf("\nFile not opened\n");

    else {

        //print heading
        printf("\nName\t\tID\t\tGPA\n\n");

        //read field information from data file and store in variables
        fscanf(pRead, "%s%s%s%f", fName, lName, id, &gpa);

        //print variable data to standard output
        printf("%s %s\t%s\t%.2f\n", fName, lName, id, gpa);
```

```
    fclose(pRead);

  }  //end if

} //end main
```

Figure 11.5 shows the output of reading the tab-delimited file created in the preceding code.

FIGURE 11.5

Reading information from a data file created by the fprintf() function.

Keep in mind that opening a data file using fopen() with a w argument value will erase any previous data stored in the file. Use the a attribute to append data at the end of the file, as discussed in the next section.

Appending Data

Appending data is a common process among Information Technology (IT) professionals because it allows programmers to continue building upon an existing file without deleting or removing previously stored data.

Appending information to a data file involves opening a data file for writing using the a attribute in an fopen() function and writing records or data to the end of an existing file. If the file does not exist, however, a new data file is created as specified in the fopen() statement.

Study the following program, which demonstrates appending records to an existing data file.

```
#include <stdio.h>

void readData(void);

main()
```

```c
{

    FILE *pWrite;
    char name[10];
    char hobby[15];

    printf("\nCurrent file contents:\n");

    readData();

    printf("\nEnter a new name and hobby: ");
    scanf("%s%s", name, hobby);

    //open data file for append
    pWrite = fopen("hobbies.dat", "a");

    if ( pWrite == NULL )

        printf("\nFile cannot be opened\n");

    else {

        //append record information to data file
        fprintf(pWrite, "%s %s\n", name, hobby);
        fclose(pWrite);
        readData();

    }   //end if

}  //end main

void readData(void)

{

    FILE *pRead;

    char name[10];
```

```
    char hobby[15];

    //open data file for read access only
    pRead = fopen("hobbies.dat", "r");

    if ( pRead == NULL )

       printf("\nFile cannot be opened\n");

    else {

       printf("\nName\tHobby\n\n");
       fscanf(pRead, "%s%s", name, hobby);

       //read records from data file until end of file is reached
       while ( !feof(pRead) ) {

          printf("%s\t%s\n", name, hobby);
          fscanf(pRead, "%s%s", name, hobby);

       }  //end loop

    }  //end if

    fclose(pRead);

}  //end readData
```

With a user-defined function called readData(), I'm able to open the hobbies.dat data file created earlier and read each record until the end-of-file is encountered. After the readData() function is finished, I prompt the user to enter another record. After successfully writing the user's new record to the data file, I once again call the readData() function to print again all records, including the one added by the user. Figure 11.6 depicts the process of appending information to data files using the preceding program.

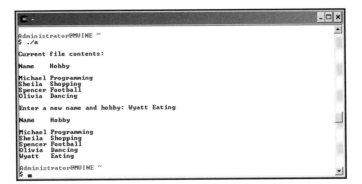

FIGURE 11.6

Appending records to a data file.

GOTO AND ERROR HANDLING

Whenever your program interacts with the outside world, you should provide some form of error handling to counteract unexpected inputs or outputs. One way of providing error handling is to write your own error-handling routines.

Error-handling routines are the traffic control for your program. Such routines should ideally consider the multitude of programming and human-generated error possibilities, resolve issues if possible, and at the very least exit the program gracefully after an error.

A BRIEF HISTORY OF GOTO

The goto keyword is a carryover from an old programming practice made popular in various languages such as BASIC, COBOL, and even C. A goto was regularly used for designing and building modularized programs. To break programs into manageable pieces, programmers would create modules and link them together using the keyword goto in hopes of simulating function calls.

After years of programming with goto, programmers began to realize that this created messy "spaghetti-like" code, which at times became nearly impossible to debug. Fortunately, improvements to the structured programming paradigm and event-driven and object-oriented programming techniques have virtually eliminated the need for goto.

Because of the lack of built-in exception handling within the C language, it is acceptable to use the once infamous goto keyword. Specifically, if you'd like to separate out error handling from each routine and save yourself from writing repetitive error handlers, then goto may be a good alternative for you.

Using `goto` is very simple: first include a label (a descriptive name) followed by a colon (`:`) above where you want your error-handling routine to run (begin). To call your error-handling routine (where you want to check for an error), simply use the keyword `goto` followed by the label name as demonstrated next.

```
int myFunction()
{
    int iReturnValue = 0;   //0 for success

  /* process something */
  if(error)
  {
      goto ErrorHandler; //go to the error-handling routine
  }
  /* do some more processing */
  if(error)
  {
      ret_val = [error];
      goto ErrorHandler; //go to the error-handling routine
  }

ErrorHandler:
    /* error-handling routine */
    return iReturnValue ;
}
```

The label in the preceding code is `ErrorHandler`, which is simply a name I came up with to identify or label my error handler. In the same sample code, you can see that I want to check for errors in each of the `if` constructs and if an error exists, I call my error handler using the keyword `goto`.

Review the next programming example, with output shown in Figure 11.7, that demonstrates the use of `goto` and a couple of new functions (`perror()` and `exit()`) to build error handling into a file I/O program.

```
#include <stdio.h>
#include <stdlib.h>

main()
```

```c
{

   FILE *pRead;
   char name[10];
   char hobby[15];

   pRead = fopen("hobbies.dat", "r");

   if ( pRead == NULL )

      goto ErrorHandler;

   else {

      printf("\nName\tHobby\n\n");
      fscanf(pRead, "%s%s", name, hobby);

      while ( !feof(pRead) ) {

         printf("%s\t%s\n", name, hobby);
         fscanf(pRead, "%s%s", name, hobby);

      }  //end loop

   } // end if

   exit(EXIT_SUCCESS); //exit program normally

   ErrorHandler:
         perror("The following error occurred");
         exit(EXIT_FAILURE); //exit program with error

} //end main
```

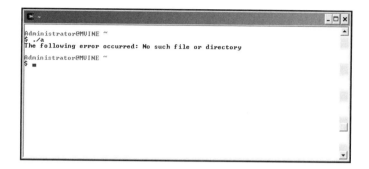

FIGURE 11.7

Using perror()
and exit()
functions to
display an error
message and exit
the program.

The exit() function, part of the <stdlib.h> library, terminates a program as if it were exited normally. As shown next, the exit() function is common with programmers who want to terminate a program when encountering file I/O (input/output) errors.

```
exit(EXIT_SUCCESS); //exit program normally
//or
exit(EXIT_FAILURE); //exit program with error
```

The exit() function takes a single parameter, a constant of either EXIT_SUCCESS or EXIT_FAILURE, both of which return a pre-defined value for success or failure, respectively.

The perror() function sends a message to standard output describing the last error encountered. The perror() function takes a single string argument, which is printed first, followed by a colon and a blank, then the system generated error message and a new line, as revealed next.

```
perror("The following error occurred");
```

CHAPTER PROGRAM—THE PHONE BOOK PROGRAM

The Phone Book program shown in Figure 11.8 uses many chapter-based concepts, including fields, records, data files, FILE pointers, and error handling, to build a simple electronic phone book. Specifically, the Phone Book program allows a user to add phone book entries and print the contents of the entire phone book.

After reading this chapter and studying the code from the Phone Book program, you should be able to build your own programs that use data files to store all kinds of information. In addition, you could build your own Phone Book program or make modifications to mine as outlined in the Challenges section.

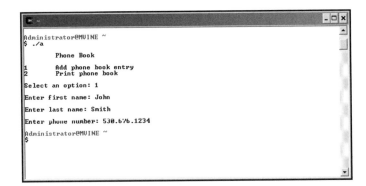

FIGURE 11.8

Appending records to a data file.

All of the code required to build the Phone Book program is revealed next.

```c
#include<stdio.h>
#include <stdlib.h>

main()

{

    int response;

    char *lName[20] = {0};
    char *fName[20] = {0};
    char *number[20] = {0};

    FILE *pWrite;
    FILE *pRead;

    printf("\n\tPhone Book\n");
    printf("\n1\tAdd phone book entry\n");
    printf("2\tPrint phone book\n\n");
    printf("Select an option: ");
    scanf("%d", &response);

    if ( response == 1 ) {

        /* user is adding a new phone book entry - get the info */
```

```c
        printf("\nEnter first name: ");
        scanf("%s", fName);
        printf("\nEnter last name: ");
        scanf("%s", lName);
        printf("\nEnter phone number: ");
        scanf("%s", number);

        pWrite = fopen("phone_book.dat", "a");

        if ( pWrite != NULL ) {

            fprintf(pWrite, "%s %s %s\n", fName, lName, number);
            fclose(pWrite);

        }

        else

            goto ErrorHandler;   //there is a file i/o error

}

else if ( response == 2 ) {

    /* user wants to print the phone book */

    pRead = fopen("phone_book.dat", "r");

    if ( pRead != NULL ) {

        printf("\nPhone Book Entries\n");

        while ( !feof(pRead) ) {

            fscanf(pRead, "%s %s %s", fName, lName, number);

            if ( !feof(pRead) )
                printf("\n%s %s\t%s", fName, lName, number);
```

```
    } //end loop

    printf("\n");

  }

  else

    goto ErrorHandler;  //there is a file i/o error

  }

  else {

    printf("\nInvalid selection\n");
  }

  exit(EXIT_SUCCESS); //exit program normally

  ErrorHandler:
      perror("The following error occurred");
      exit(EXIT_FAILURE); //exit program with error

} //end main
```

SUMMARY

- Data files are often text-based and are used for storing and retrieving related information like that stored in a database.
- Also known as binary digits, bits are the smallest value in a data file; each bit value can only be a 0 or 1.
- Bits are the smallest unit of measurement in computer systems.
- Bytes are most commonly made up of eight bits and are used to store a single character, such as a number, a letter, or any other character found in a character set.
- Groupings of characters are referred to as fields.
- Records are logical groupings of fields that comprise a single row of information.
- Data files are comprised of one or more records.

- Use an internal data structure called FILE to point to and manage a file stream in C.
- To open a data file, use the standard input/output library function fopen().
- The fclose() function uses the FILE pointer to flush the stream and close the file.
- The fscanf() function is similar to the scanf() function but works with FILE streams and takes three arguments: a FILE pointer, a data type, and a variable to store the retrieved value in.
- To test when an end-of-file marker is reached, pass the FILE pointer to the feof() function and loop until the function returns a non-zero value.
- The fprintf() function takes a FILE pointer, a list of data types, and a list of values (or variables) to write information to a data file.
- Appending information to a data file involves opening a data file for writing using the a attribute in an fopen() function and writing records or data to the end of an existing file.
- The keyword goto is used to simulate function calls and can be leveraged to build error-handling routines.
- The exit() function terminates a program.
- The perror() function sends a message to standard output describing the last error encountered.

CHALLENGES

1. Create a data file called `friends.dat` using any text-based editor and enter at least three records storing your friends' first and last names. Make sure that each field in the record is separated by a white space.

2. Using the `friends.dat` file from challenge number one, build another program that uses the `fscanf()` function for reading each record and printing field information to standard output until the end-of-file is reached. Include an error-handling routine that notifies the user of any system errors and exits the program.

3. Create a program that uses a menu with options to enter student information (name, ID, GPA), print student information, or quit the program. Use data files and `FILE` pointers to store and print information entered.

4. Modify the Phone Book program to allow the user to enter multiple entries without quitting the program.

5. Continue to modify the Phone Book program to allow a user to modify or delete phone book entries.

THE C PREPROCESSOR

Understanding the C preprocessor is an important step in learning how to build large programs with multiple files. In this chapter I will show you how to break your C programs into separate files and use the gcc compiler to link and compile those files into a single working executable software program. Moreover, you will learn about preprocessor techniques and concepts such as symbolic constants, macros, function headers, and definition files.

Specifically, this chapter covers the following topics:

- Introduction to the C preprocessor
- Symbolic constants
- Creating and using macros
- Building larger programs

INTRODUCTION TO THE C PREPROCESSOR

C programs must go through a number of steps before an executable file can be created. The most common of these steps are performed by the preprocessor, compiler, and linker, which are orchestrated by software programs such as gcc. As discussed in Chapter 1, "Getting Started with C Programming," the gcc program performs the following actions to create an executable file.

1. Preprocesses program code and looks for various directives.
2. Generates error codes and messages.
3. Compiles program code into object code and stores temporarily on disk.
4. Links any necessary library to the object code and creates an executable file stored on disk.

In this chapter, I will concentrate primarily on preprocessing, which generally involves reading specialized statements called *preprocessor directives*. Preprocessor directives are often found littered through C source files (source files end with a .c extension) and can serve many common and useful functions. Specifically, ANSI C preprocessors, such as the one found in gcc, can insert or replace text and organize source code through conditional compilation. The type of preprocessor directive encountered dictates each of these functions.

Believe it or not, you are already familiar with preprocessor directives. To demonstrate, consider the C library header files `<stdio.h>` and `<string.h>`, which are commonly typed at the beginning of C programs. To use library functions defined in header files, such as `printf()` or `scanf()`, you must tell the C preprocessor to include the specific header file or files using a preprocessor directive called `#include`.

A simple program that uses this preprocessor directive is shown next.

```
#include <stdio.h>


main()


{


    printf("\nHaving fun with preprocessor directives\n");


}
```

The pound (#) sign is a special preprocessor character that is used to direct the preprocessor to perform some action. In fact, all preprocessor directives are prefaced with the # symbol. Moreover, you might be surprised to learn that the preprocessor has its own language that can be used to build symbolic constants and macros.

Symbolic Constants

Symbolic constants are easy to understand. In fact, symbolic constants are similar in application to the constant data type you learned about in Chapter 2, "Primary Data Types." Like other preprocessor directives, symbolic constants must be created outside of any function.

In addition, symbolic constants must be preceded by a #define preprocessor directive, as shown next.

```
#define NUMBER 7
```

When the preprocessor encounters a symbolic constant name, in this case NUMBER, it replaces all occurrences of the constant name found in the source code with its definition, in this case 7. Remember, this is a preprocessor directive, so the process of text replacement occurs before your program is compiled into an executable file. Refer to the following program and its output in Figure 12.1 for an example of how symbolic constants work.

```
#include <stdio.h>

#define NUMBER 7

main()

{

    printf("\nLucky Number %d\n", NUMBER);

}
```

FIGURE 12.1

Demonstrating preprocessor directives using symbolic constants.

You should follow two rules when working with symbolic constants. First, always capitalize symbolic constants so that they are easy to spot in your program code. Second, do not attempt to reassign data to symbolic constants, as demonstrated next.

```
#include <stdio.h>

#define NUMBER 7

main()

{

    printf("\nLucky Number %d\n", NUMBER);

    NUMBER = 5;    //can not do this

}
```

Attempting to change a symbolic constant's value will prevent your program from success-fully compiling, as Figure 12.2 reveals.

FIGURE 12.2

Attempting to change the value of a symbolic constant generates a compiler error.

ARE PREPROCESSOR DIRECTIVES C STATEMENTS?

Preprocessor directives are actions performed before the compiler begins its job. Preprocessor directives act only to change the source program before the source code is compiled. The reason semicolons are not used is because they are not C statements and they are not executed during a program's execution. In the case of #include, the preprocessor directive expands the source code so the compiler sees a much larger source program when it finally gets to do its job.

Creating and Using Macros

Macros provide another interesting investigation into preprocessor text replacement. In fact, C preprocessors treat macros similarly to symbolic constants—they use text-replacement techniques and are created with the #define statement.

Macros provide a useful shortcut to tasks that are performed frequently. For example, consider the following formula that computes the area of a rectangle.

```
Area of a rectangle = length x width
```

If the area values of length and width were always 10 and 5, you could build a macro like this:

```
#define AREA 10 * 5
```

In the real world, however, you know that this would be very limiting if not useless. Macros can play a greater role when built to use incoming and outgoing variables like a user-defined function would. When built in this way, macros can save a C programmer keyboard time when using easily repeated statements. To demonstrate, study the next program that improves the area of a rectangle formula.

```
#include <stdio.h>
#define AREA(l,w) ( l * w )

main()

{

   int length = 0;
   int width = 0;

   printf("\nEnter length: ");
   scanf("%d", &length);
   printf("\nEnter width: ");
   scanf("%d", &width);

   printf("\nArea of rectangle = %d\n", AREA(length,width));
}
```

Figure 12.3 demonstrates a sample output from the preceding program, which uses a macro to determine the area of a rectangle.

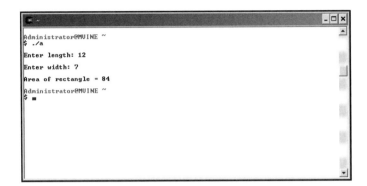

FIGURE 12.3

Using a macro to calculate the area of a rectangle.

As you can see in Figure 12.3, the macro acts similarly to any C library or user-defined function—it takes arguments and returns values. The C preprocessor has replaced the reference of the AREA macro inside the main() function with the macro definition defined outside of the main() function. Once again, this all happens prior to compiling (creating) an executable file.

Take a closer look at the macro definition again:

```
#define AREA(l,w) ( l * w )
```

The first part of this macro defines its name, AREA. The next sequence of characters (l,w) tells the preprocessor that this macro will receive two arguments. The last part of the AREA macro (l * w) explains to the preprocessor what the macro will do. The preprocessor does not perform the macro's calculation. Instead, it replaces any reference to the name AREA in source files with the macro's definition.

You may be surprised to find out that besides simple numerical computation, macros can contain library functions such as printf(), as shown in the next program (with output shown in Figure 12.4).

```
#include <stdio.h>

#define RESULT(x,y) ( printf("\nResult is %d\n", x+y) )

main()

{

    int num1 = 0;
    int num2 = 0;
```

```
printf("\nEnter first number: ");
scanf("%d", & num1);
printf("\nEnter second number: ");
scanf("%d", & num2);

RESULT(num1, num2);

}
```

FIGURE 12.4

Using the
printf()
function inside a
macro definition.

Figure 12.4 demonstrates that you can easily use library functions inside macro definitions. Remember: do not use a semicolon in the macro definition. Take another look at the macro definition I used.

```
#define RESULT(x,y) ( printf("\nResult is %d\n", x+y) )
```

I didn't use a semicolon to end the statement within the macro definition or to end the macro itself because the gcc compiler would have returned a parse error, which happens to be the line number at which I reference the RESULT macro. But why at the line where I reference the macro and not the line at which the macro is defined? Remember, the preprocessor replaces text with references to #define preprocessor directives; when it attempts to replace the RESULT reference, the source code for the main() function might look something like this.

```
main()

{

    int operand1 = 0;
    int operand2 = 0;
```

```
printf("\nEnter first operand: ");
scanf("%d", &operand1);
printf("\nEnter second operand: ");
scanf("%d", &operand2);

/* The following macro reference... */
RESULT(num1, num2);
/* ...might be replaced with this: */
printf("\nResult is %d\n", x+y);;   //notice the extra semicolon

}
```

Notice the extra semicolon in the last printf() function. Because a semicolon was used in the macro definition and in the macro call, two semicolons were processed by the compiler, potentially creating a parse error.

BUILDING LARGER PROGRAMS

In Chapter 5, "Structured Programming," I touched on the concept of breaking large problems into smaller, more manageable ones using structured programming techniques such as top-down design and functions. In this section, I will show you how you can extend those concepts by splitting your programs into separate program files using preprocessor directives, header files, and gcc.

Dividing a program into separate files allows you to easily reuse your components (functions) and provides an environment where multiple programmers can work simultaneously on the same software application. You already know that structured programming involves breaking problems into manageable components. So far, you have learned how to do so by dividing your tasks into components that are built with function prototypes and headers. With this knowledge and the understanding of how the C preprocessor works with multiple files, you will find it easy to divide your programs into separate file entities.

Consider the preprocessor directive #include <stdio.h>. This directive tells the C preprocessor to include the standard input output library with your program during the linking process. Moreover, the <stdio.h> library consists primarily of function headers or prototypes, thus the .h extension. The actual function implementations or definitions for the standard input output library are stored in a completely different file called stdio.c. It is not required to include this file in your programs because the gcc compiler automatically knows where to find this file based on the associated header file and predefined directory structure.

You can easily build your own header and definition files using your knowledge of functions and a few new techniques. To prove this, consider a simple program that calculates a profit. To calculate a profit, use the following equation.

```
Profit = (price)(quantity sold) - total cost
```

I will decompose a program to calculate a profit into three separate files:

- Function header file—profit.h
- Function definition file—profit.c
- Main function—main.c

Header File

Header files end with an .h extension and contain function prototypes including various data types and/or constants required by the functions. To build the function header file for my profit program, I'll create a new file called profit.h and place the following function prototype in it.

```
void profit(float, float, float);
```

Because I'm using a single user-defined function in my profit program, the preceding statement is the only code required in my header file. I could have created this file in any text editing program such as vi, nano, or Microsoft Notepad.

Function Definition File

Function definition files contain all the code required to implement function prototypes found in corresponding header files. After building my header file with the required function prototype, I can begin work on creating its corresponding function definition file, which is called profit.c.

For the profit program, my function implementation will look like the following:

```
void profit(float p, float q, float tc)

{

   printf("\nYour profit is %.2f\n", (p * q) - tc);

}
```

At this point I've created two separate files: profit.h for my function prototype and profit.c for my function implementation. Keep in mind that neither of these files have been compiled—more on this in a moment.

main() Function File

Now that I've built both function header and definition files, I can concentrate on creating my main program file where I will pull everything together with the help of the C preprocessor. All of the code required to build the profit program's main() function is revealed next.

```c
#include <stdio.h>
#include "profit.h"


main()


{

    float price, totalCost;
    int quantity;

    printf("\nThe Profit Program\n");
    printf("\nEnter unit price: ");
    scanf("%f", &price);

    printf("Enter quantity sold: ");
    scanf("%d", &quantity);

    printf("Enter total cost: ");
    scanf("%f", &totalCost);

    profit(price,quantity,totalCost);

} //end main
```

All of the program code stored in main.c and is pretty straightforward and should be familiar to you, with one exception shown next.

```c
#include <stdio.h>
#include "profit.h"
```

The first preprocessor directive tells the C preprocessor to find and include the standard input output library header file. Surrounding a header file in an #include statement with the less than (<) and greater than (>) symbols tells the C preprocessor to look in a predefined installation directory. The second #include statement also tells the C preprocessor to include a header file; this time, however, I've used double quotes to surround my own header file name. Using double quotes in this fashion tells the C preprocessor to look for the header file in the same directory as the file being compiled.

Pulling It All Together

Speaking of compiling, it's now time pull all of these files together using gcc. Pass all definition files ending in .c, separated by a space, to the gcc compiler to properly link and compile a program that uses multiple files, as demonstrated in Figure 12.5.

FIGURE 12.5

Using gcc to link multiple files.

After preprocessing directives, linking multiple files, and compiling, gcc produces a single working executable file demonstrated in Figure 12.6.

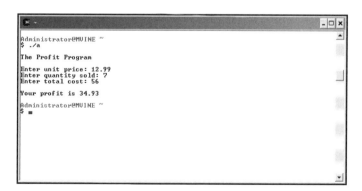

FIGURE 12.6

Demonstrating the output of a program built with multiple files.

CHAPTER PROGRAM—THE FUNCTION WIZARD

Shown in Figure 12.7, the Function Wizard uses multiple files to build a single program that calculates the following rectangle-based functions:

- Determine perimeter of a rectangle
- Determine area of a rectangle
- Determine volume of a rectangle

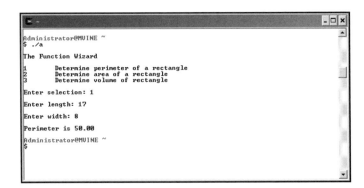

FIGURE 12.7

Using chapter-based concepts to build the Function Wizard program.

All program code for each file in the Function Wizard is listed next in its appropriate section.

ch12_calculate.h

The header file ch12_calculate.h lists three function prototypes that calculate the perimeter, area, and volume of a rectangle.

```
void perimeter(float, float);
void area(float, float);
void volume(float, float, float);
```

ch12_calculate.c

The function definition file ch12_calculate.c implements the three rectangle functions prototyped in ch12_calculate.h.

```
#include <stdio.h>

void perimeter(float l, float w)

{
```

```
    printf("\nPerimeter is %.2f\n", (2*l) + (2*w));

}

void area(float l, float w)

{

    printf("\nArea is %.2f\n", l * w);

}

void volume(float l, float w, float h)

{

    printf("\nThe volume is %.2f\n", l * w * h);

}
```

ch12_main.c

The main program file ch12_main.c allows the user to calculate the perimeter, area, and volume of a rectangle. Notice the inclusion of the header file ch12_header.h, which contains the rectangle-based function prototypes.

```
#include <stdio.h>
#include "ch12_calculate.h"

main()

{

    int selection = 0;
    float l,w,h;

    printf("\nThe Function Wizard\n");
    printf("\n1\tDetermine perimeter of a rectangle\n");
    printf("2\tDetermine area of a rectangle\n");
```

```c
printf("3\tDetermine volume of rectangle\n");
printf("\nEnter selection: ");
scanf("%d", &selection);

switch (selection) {

    case 1:

        printf("\nEnter length: ");
        scanf("%f", &l);
        printf("\nEnter width: ");
        scanf("%f", &w);
        perimeter(l,w);
        break;

    case 2:

        printf("\nEnter length: ");
        scanf("%f", &l);
        printf("\nEnter width: ");
        scanf("%f", &w);
        area(l,w);
        break;

    case 3:

        printf("\nEnter length: ");
        scanf("%f", &l);
        printf("\nEnter width: ");
        scanf("%f", &w);
        printf("\nEnter height: ");
        scanf("%f", &h);
        volume(l,w,h);
        break;

    }  // end switch

}  // end main
```

SUMMARY

- The pound (#) sign is a special preprocessor character that is used to direct the preprocessor to perform some action.

- Symbolic constants must be created outside of any function and must be preceded by a #define preprocessor directive.

- Attempting to change a symbolic constant's value will prevent your program from successfully compiling.

- Preprocessor directives are not implemented with C syntax and, therefore, do not require the use of a semicolon after program statements. Inserting a semicolon at the end of a preprocessor directive will cause a parse error during compilation.

- Macros provide a useful shortcut to tasks that are performed frequently.

- Macros can contain library functions such as printf().

- Dividing a program into separate files allows you to easily reuse your components (functions) and provides an environment where multiple programmers can work simultaneously on the same software application.

- Header files end with an .h extension and contain function prototypes including various data types and/or constants required by the functions.

- Function definition files contain all the code required to implement function prototypes found in corresponding header files.

- Using double quotes to surround a header file name tells the C preprocessor to look for the header file in the same directory as the file being compiled.

- Pass all definition files ending in .c, separated by a space, to the gcc compiler to properly link and compile a program that uses multiple files.

CHALLENGES

1. Build a program that creates a macro to calculate the area of a circle using the formula area = $\pi \cdot r^2$ (area = pie x radius x radius). In the same program, prompt the user to enter a circle's radius. Use the macro to calculate the circle's area and display the result to the user.

2. Build a simple program that prompts a user to input the length and width of a rectangle using a macro to calculate the perimeter. After retrieving the length and width, pass the data as arguments in a call to the macro. Use the following algorithm to derive the perimeter of a rectangle.

```
Perimeter of a rectangle = 2(length) + 2 (width)
```
3. **Use a similar program design as in Challenge I that uses a macro to calculate total revenue. Use the following formula to calculate total revenue.**
    ```
    Total revenue = (price)(quantity)
    ```
4. **Modify the Function Wizard program to include the following function.**
    ```
    Average cost = total cost / quantity
    ```
5. **Divide the Cryptogram program from Chapter 7, "Pointers," into multiple files using chapter-based concepts.**

What's Next?

C is not an easy programming language to learn, so you should feel a sense of accomplishment in learning in what is considered one of the most challenging and powerful programming languages ever developed.

If you haven't done so already, create programs to solve the challenges at the end of each chapter. I can't emphasize enough that the only way to learn how to program is to program. It's just like learning a spoken language; you can get only so much from reading and listening. Speaking a language regularly is the key to learning it, and in this case programming is the key to learning the C language.

If you're still hungry for more C, I recommend reviewing Appendix E, "Common C Library Functions." There will you find a number of useful functions to explore. If you are seeking advanced challenges with C, I recommend studying advanced data structures such as linked lists, stacks, queues, and trees.

Another natural progression for C programming students is learning how to develop Graphical User Interfaces (GUIs) for a Windows-like environment. In today's world, GUI's are often built using object-oriented programming languages with syntax similar to that of C such as C++, C#, or even Java, all of which require a study of the object-oriented programming (OOP) paradigm.

You can find a wealth of information about these topics and more by searching the Internet or visiting our Web site at http://www.courseptr.com for more great programming books. Good luck, best wishes, and keep programming!

Michael Vine.

APPENDIX A

COMMON UNIX COMMANDS

Command Name	Functionality
>	Redirection operator—writes data to a file
>>	Append operator—appends data to a file
--help	Displays help information for some shell commands
cd	Changes directory
chmod	Changes file codes (permissions)
cp	Copies files
echo	Directs text to standard output device (computer screen)
history	Shows previously used shell commands
kill	Terminates a process
ls	Lists the contents of a directory
man	Displays manual pages for various shell commands
mkdir	Creates a directory
mv	Moves or renames files
ps	Displays process information
pwd	Prints working directory
rm	Removes files
rmdir	Removes a directory

TABLE A.1   COMMON UNIX COMMANDS

VIM QUICK GUIDE

V IM is an improved version of the popular UNIX text editor vi (pronounced "vee-eye"). For the most part, commands found in vi are available in VIM and vice versa.

Using the escape (Esc) key to switch between modes, VIM operates in two distinct forms: insert and command mode. In insert mode, you type characters to construct a document or program. Command mode, however, takes keys pressed and translates them into various functions. The most common frustration of new VIM users is the distinction between these two modes.

To start VIM, simply type in **VI** or **VIM** from your UNIX command prompt. Typing VI from the command prompt will launch VIM. Figure B.1 depicts the opening VIM screen.

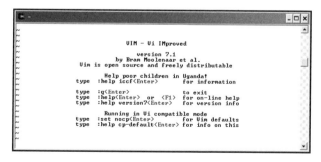

FIGURE B.1

The opening VIM screen.

VIM contains a very good user's guide and help system, so without re-inventing the wheel I'll show you how to navigate through the built-in VIM help files and user guides.

From within the VIM screen, type the following:

`:help`

The colon in front of the word `help` is required; essentially it tells VIM that you're entering a command.

As shown in Figure B.2, you can use the arrow keys to navigate through the help file. After viewing the help file, you may notice a list of other files for viewing. You might want to open a second Cygwin shell and start another VIM session so that you can practice along with the VIM user's guide.

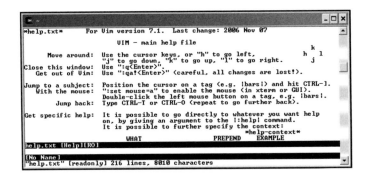

FIGURE B.2

The VIM help screen.

I recommend viewing and working through the following files:

- `usr_01.txt`
- `usr_02.txt`
- `usr_03.txt`
- `usr_04.txt`

When you're ready to start viewing the next file (`usr_01.txt`), simply type the following from the help screen:

`:help usr_01.txt`

From each of the user document screens, follow the aforementioned pattern to gain access to the next user document.

APPENDIX

NANO QUICK GUIDE

A free UNIX-based text editor, nano is similar to its less enabled cousin Pico. nano is an easy-to-use and easy-to-learn UNIX text editor with which you can write text files and programs in languages such as Java, C++, and, of course, C.

To start a nano process, simply type the word nano at your Cygwin UNIX command prompt (see Figure C.1). If you're using another UNIX shell other than Cygwin, you may not have access to nano. In this case, you can use the common UNIX editor Pico, which shares many of nano's capabilities and command structures.

FIGURE C.1

The free nano
UNIX text editor.

Unlike VIM or vi, nano operates under one mode. Its single base mode of operation makes it an excellent candidate for beginning UNIX users, but prevents the existence of many advanced text editing features found in VIM or vi.

To create a new text file (C program, letter, memo, etc.) simply start typing from nano's interface.

nano has two categories of program options. The first category of options is used when first launching the nano program. For example, the following code launches nano with an option to constantly show the cursor position.

```
$ nano −c
```

Table C.1 shows a comprehensive list of nano start options. This list is derived from the free nano help facility accessed from its corresponding man pages.

TABLE C.1	NANO START OPTIONS

Option	Description
-T	Sets tab width
-R	Enables regular expression matching for search strings
-V	Shows the current version and author
-h	Displays command line options
-c	Constantly shows the cursor position
-i	Indents new lines to the previous line's indentation
-k	Enables cut from cursor to end of line with Ctrl K
-l	Replaces symbolic link with a new file
-m	Enables mouse support if available
-p	Emulates Pico
-r	Wraps lines at column number
-s	Enables alternative spell checker command
-t	Always saves changed buffer without prompting
-v	Views file in read only mode
-w	Disables wrapping of long lines
-x	Disables help screen at bottom of editor
-z	Enables suspend ability
+LINE	Places cursor at LINE on startup

Once inside the nano editor, you can use a number of commands to help you edit your text file. Most of nano's command structures can be accessed using control-key sequences denoted by the carrot character (^), function keys, or through meta keys (Esc or Alt keys). Table C.2 describes the most common nano commands as found in the Get Help feature.

TABLE C.2	COMMON NANO COMMANDS	
Control-Key Sequence	**Optional Key**	**Description**
^G	F1	Invokes the help menu
^X	F2	Exits nano
^O	F3	Writes current file to disk (save)
^R	F5	Inserts new file into the current one
^\		Replaces text within the editor
^W	F6	Searches for text
^Y	F7	Moves to the previous screen
^V	F8	Moves to the next screen
^K	F9	Cuts current line and store in buffer
^U	F10	Uncuts from buffer into current line
^C	F11	Shows the cursor position
^T	F12	Invokes spell checker if available
^P		Moves up one line
^N		Moves down one line
^F		Moves forward one character
^B		Moves back one character
^A		Moves to beginning of current line
^E		Moves to end of current line
^L		Refreshes screen
^^		Marks text at current cursor location
^D		Deletes character under cursor
^H		Deletes character to left of cursor
^I		Inserts tab character
^J	F4	Justifies current paragraph
^M		Inserts carriage return at cursor

Common ASCII Character Codes

Code	Character
0	NUL (null)
1	SOH (start of heading)
2	STX (start of text)
3	ETX (end of text)
4	EOT (end of transmission)
5	ENQ (enquiry)
6	ACK (acknowledge)
7	BEL (bell)
8	BS (backspace)
9	TAB (horizontal tab)
10	LF (new line)
11	VT (vertical tab)
12	FF (form feed, new page)
13	CR (carriage return)
14	SO (shift out)
15	SI (shift in)
16	DLE (data link escape)
17	DC1 (device control 1)

Code	Character
18	DC2 (device control 2)
19	DC3 (device control 3)
20	DC4 (device control 4)
21	NAK (negative acknowledge)
22	SYN (synchronous idle)
23	ETB (end of transmission block)
24	CAN (cancel)
25	EM (end of medium)
26	SUB (substitute)
27	ESC (escape)
28	FS (file separator)
29	GS (group separator)
30	RS (record separator)
31	US (unit separator)
32	Space
33	!
34	"
35	#
36	$
37	%
38	&
39	'
40	(
41	)
42	*
43	+
44	,
45	—
46	.
47	/
48	0
49	1
50	2
51	3
52	4
53	5
54	6
55	7
56	8

Code	Character
57	9
58	:
59	;
60	<
61	=
62	>
63	?
64	@
65	A
66	B
67	C
68	D
69	E
70	F
71	G
72	H
73	I
74	J
75	K
76	L
77	M
78	N
79	O
80	P
81	Q
82	R
83	S
84	T
85	U
86	V
87	W
88	X
89	Y
90	Z
91	[
92	\
93	]
94	^

Code	Character
95	—
96	`
97	a
98	b
99	c
100	d
101	e
102	f
103	g
104	h
105	i
106	j
107	k
108	l
109	m
110	n
111	o
112	p
113	q
114	r
115	s
116	t
117	u
118	v
119	w
120	x
121	y
122	z
123	{
124	|
125	}
126	~
127	DEL (Delete)

APPENDIX

Common C Library Functions

The following tables represent some of the more common C Library functions grouped by their corresponding library header file.

| TABLE E.1 | CTYPE.H |

Function Name	Description
isalnum()	Determines if a character is alphanumeric (A–Z, a–z, 0–9).
iscntrl()	Determines if a character is a control or delete character.
isdigit()	Determines if a character is a digit (0–9).
isgraph()	Determines if a character is printable, excluding the space (decimal 32).
islower()	Determines if a character is a lowercase letter (a–z).
isprint()	Determines if a character is printable (decimal 32–126).
ispunct()	Determines if a character is punctuation (decimal 32–47, 58–63, 91–96, 123–126).
isspace()	Determines if a character is white space.
isupper()	Determines if a character is an uppercase letter (A–Z).
isxdigit()	Determines if a character is hex digit (0–9, A–F, a–f).
toupper()	Converts a lowercase character to uppercase.
tolower()	Converts an uppercase character to lowercase.
isascii()	Determines if the parameter is between 0 and 127.
toascii()	Converts a character to ASCII.

TABLE E.2 MATH.H

Function Name	Description
acos()	Arccosine.
asin()	Arcsine.
atan()	Arctangent.
atan2()	Arctangent function of two variables.
ceil()	Smallest integral value not less than x.
cos()	Cosine.
cosh()	Hyperbolic cosine.
exp()	Exponential.
log()	Logarithmic.
pow()	Computes a value taken to an exponent.
fabs()	Absolute value of floating-point number.
floor()	Largest integral value not greater than x.
fmod()	Floating-point remainder.
frexp()	Converts floating-point number to fractional and integral components.
ldexp()	Multiplies floating-point number by integral power of 2.
modf()	Extracts signed integral and fractional values from floating-point number.
sin()	The sine of an integer.
sinh()	Hyperbolic sine.
sqrt()	Square root of a number.
tan()	Tangent.
tanh()	Hyperbolic tangent.

TABLE E.3   STDIO.H

Function Name	Description
clearerr()	Clears the end-of-file and error indicators.
fclose()	Closes a file.
feof()	Checks for EOF while reading a file.
fflush()	Flushes a stream.
fgetc()	Reads a character from a file.
fgets()	Reads a record from a file.
fopen()	Opens a file for reading or writing.
fprintf()	Outputs a line of data to a file.
fputc()	Puts a character into a file.
fputs()	Puts a string into a file.
fread()	Binary stream input.
freopen()	Opens a file for reading or writing.
fseek()	Repositions a file stream.
ftell()	Obtains current file position indicator.
fwrite()	Binary stream output.
getc()	Retrieves a character from an input stream.
getchar()	Retrieves a character from the keyboard (STDIN).
gets()	Retrieves string (from keyboard).
perror()	Prints a system error message.
printf()	Outputs data to the screen or a file.
putchar()	Outputs a character to STDOUT.
puts()	Outputs data to the screen or a file (stdout).
remove()	Removes a file.
rename()	Renames a file.
rewind()	Repositions the file indicator to the beginning of a file.
scanf()	Input format conversion.
fscanf()	Input format conversion.
setbuf()	Provides stream buffering operations.
sprintf()	Outputs data in the same way as printf but puts into a string.
sscanf()	Extracts fields from a string.
tmpfile()	Creates a temporary file.
tmpnam()	Creates a name for a temporary file.

TABLE E.4 STDLIB.H

Function Name	Description
abort()	Aborts a program.
abs()	Computes the absolute value of an integer.
atexit()	Executes the named function when the program terminates.
atof()	Converts a string to a double.
atoi()	Accepts +-0123456789 leading blanks and converts to integer.
atol()	Converts a string to a long integer.
bsearch()	Binary searches an array.
calloc()	Allocates memory for an array.
div()	Computes the quotient and remainder of integer division.
exit()	Terminates a program normally.
getenv()	Gets an environmental variable.
free()	Frees memory allocated with malloc().
labs()	Computes the absolute value of a long integer.
ldiv()	Computes the quotient and remainder of long integer division.
malloc()	Dynamically allocates memory.
mblen()	Determines the number of bytes in a character.
mbstowcs()	Converts a multibyte string to a wide character string.
mbtowc()	Converts a multibyte character to a wide character.
qsort()	Sorts an array.
rand()	Generates a random number.
realloc()	Reallocates memory.
strtod()	Converts a string to a double.
strtol()	Converts string to long integer.
strtoul()	Converts a string to an unsigned long.
srand()	Seeds a random number.
system()	Issues a command to the operating system.
wctomb()	Converts a wide character to a multibyte character.
wcstombs()	Converts a wide character string to a multibyte character string.

TABLE E.5   STRING.H

Function Name	Description
memchr()	Copies a character into memory.
memcmp()	Compares memory locations.
memcpy()	Copies n bytes between areas of memory.
memmove()	Copies n bytes between areas of potentially overlapping memory.
memset()	Sets memory.
strcat()	Concatenates two strings.
strchr()	Searches for a character in a string.
strcmp()	Compares two strings.
strcoll()	Compares two strings using the current locale's collating order.
strcpy()	Copies a string from one location to another.
strcspn()	Searches a string for a set of characters.
strerror()	Returns the string representation of errno.
strlen()	Returns the length of a string.
strncat()	Concatenates two strings.
strncmp()	Compares two strings.
strncpy()	Copies part of a string.
strpbrk()	Finds characters in a string.
strrchr()	Searches for a character in a string.
strspn()	Searches a string for a set of characters.
strstr()	Searches a string for a substring.
strtok()	Parses a string into a sequence of tokens.

TABLE E.6   TIME.H

Function Name	Description
asctime()	Converts time to a string.
clock()	Returns an approximation of processor time used by the program.
ctime()	Converts a time value to string in the same format as asctime.
difftime()	Returns the difference in seconds between two times.
gmtime()	Converts time to Coordinated Universal Time (UTC).
localtime()	Converts time to local time.
mktime()	Converts time to a time value.
strftime()	Formats date and time.
time()	Returns time in seconds.

INDEX